SEND ME A POSTCARD

Frances Flynn

SEND ME A POSTCARD

A Memoir of the Sea

Frances Flynn

SEND ME A POSTCARD

International Standard Book Number: 0-942323-28-9
Library of Congress Catalog Number: 98-66048

Cover Design by Sheldon A. Larson

Published by
North American Heritage Press
A DIVISION OF
CREATIVE MEDIA, INC.
P.O. Box 1
Minot, North Dakota 58702, USA
701-852-5552

Printed in the United States of America

To

Rachel, Sonia,
Michelle, Ashley, James
and Laura

❤ ❤ ❤ ❤ ❤ ❤

Acknowledgments

Five times I have boarded Norwegian Freighters that ply the Atlantic. Meeting people of diverse cultures is much to my liking and people are wonderful. I have been lucky to meet people from four continents and fourteen countries. These include Australia, South America, Europe, and North America. Countries include Norway, England, Germany, France, Spain, Canada, USA, Mexico, Brazil, Uruguay, Argentina, Chile, Colombia, Western Australia and the Ukraine.

Many have shared with me their backgrounds, travels, hopes, dreams, failures and successes. I treasure the memories and confidences. I warmly thank all these gracious folks who didn't even know they were lifting me up.

I am grateful to Barb Swenson who offered to help get this story together. She asked for nothing in return. I would also like to thank Luther Bjerke for building my confidence and the encouragement he gave to me in getting this book published.

Table of Contents

CHAPTER I

Aboard the MV Santa Fe

February 1992

—

April 1992

MV Santa Fe

Sails from United States to Buenos Aires. Carries 500 to 700 containers and 12 passengers. The round trip is about 54 days and costs $6,000 per passenger.

SHIP'S LOG

We made a decision.

We were very lucky!

The cab driver was entertaining.

We had to put on life jackets.

Chapter I

February 1992

My husband Charles and I have been asked many times how we came to take this trip. For several years we had talked of taking a freighter. There was an ad in the Wall Street Journal of a travel agency called Freighter World Cruises. We ordered information, talked by telephone to an agent and made a decision. We wanted:

1. A Norwegian registered freighter.

2. A destination down the east coast of South America.

3. A freighter that carried only a few passengers.

We chose a Norwegian freighter named Santa Fe, owned by the Ivaran Shipping Company headquartered in Oslo, Norway. This company also has an office in New Jersey. We were very lucky to have chosen this ship.

Tampico, Mexico

I believe it is February 28th but do not have a calendar. My writing suffers from the sway of the ship but that is not important here. Now I must back up a bit. We flew out of Fargo, ND, February 23rd. There was a short stop in Denver and arrived in Houston, Texas around 11:00 p.m. We took a taxi to our hotel. The cab driver was very entertaining and gave us a smattering of Texas history.

The ship sailed February 26th. There is a fifty-mile-long channel that was dredged for sea-going vessels. When we left the channel for the open sea, we sped along

SHIP'S LOG

in calm beautiful water. Yesterday we had a fire drill. We had to put on life jackets and rush to a life boat that carries twenty-five people. The boat is stocked for emergencies and is completely enclosed. There is one lifeboat on the port side of the ship and one on the starboard side. We are assigned the one on port.

The Captain is a tall, handsome Norwegian and the Chief Steward is sparkly and quite a charmer. Last night there was a welcome aboard party. All officers and crew wore black slacks and white shirts. Dress is very casual which is lucky for me since I have no satin, lace or sequined gowns. The day we boarded this vessel there was much food and wine. So much I cannot name it.

There was much food and wine.

There are ten other passengers. Two older Jewish ladies from Cincinnati, a friendly couple from Florida, a couple from Memphis, an ex-school teacher from British Columbia, a woman from New Jersey, a man from Hiltonhead, Carolina and a woman from Jacksonville, Florida.

As I write we are in the harbor of Tampico, Mexico. The freight containers are being unloaded and new containers will be loaded. I have no idea what the containers contain. Just a bit of a surprise, we are returning to Houston and then the long trip will begin. The Captain says we will have a humdinger of a party when we cross the Equator. That is a few days from now. So far the sailing has been smooth.

The sailing has been smooth.

A pretty, young woman named Olga comes to the cabin to tidy up. I'm not used to being waited on like this and tell her I can easily do the housekeeping chores but she answers there would not be enough for her to do if I did her work. These stewardesses work hard, cleaning and serving food.

I'm not used to being waited on like this.

SHIP'S LOG

A lot of closet space.

Sea water is hard on paint.

Just like a taxi, it's sometimes hard to get a tug boat.

Some of the passengers went into Tampico to look it over. I preferred to stay on board and read, write, and wander about. Charles, too, went to town. They saw a few carts pulled by donkeys and not much for shopping. Most of these passengers are quite wealthy by my standards. They have traveled many places and taken many cruises.

Our cabin is very well furnished. We have two beds, a lot of closet space, writing desk, couch, bathroom, and drawers. There is a refrigerator, telephone for ship calls, and a television which does not work unless we are near shore.

We are told when we get to Buenos Aires the ship will go into dry dock for a week for small repairs and some painting. Sea water is hard on paint. We will be housed in a hotel and Ivaran Lines pays for all of it, including fifty dollars each a day for a food allowance. Any shopping or entertainment costs, we pay.

There are many paper back books to read. I didn't know if there would be books and I brought along a lot of them.

Saturday – February 29, 1992

We are sailing from Tampico back to Houston. We were to leave last night at ten p.m. but could not get a tug boat to tow us out of the harbor. We are sailing in the Gulf. When we get to Houston and sail south again, we will have crossed the Gulf three times. Water is smooth. My hair gets frizzier the longer we are at sea.

Monday – March 2, 1992

Yesterday a woman named Mollie taught me how to play gin rummy. Not a very difficult game. I'm no hot card player. A lot of my time is spent reading and have

I sleep well with the motion.

We are served potatoes, other dishes, potatoes, other dishes, potatoes, other dishes.

One officer was swearing in Norwegian until I translated it.

now finished two books. Charles wanders about looking for anyone to visit. We have been away from home a whole week and are still in Houston harbor.

The trip to Tampico took twenty-four hours each way. The Captain wants to leave here this evening but there are many more containers to load. There are ships in this harbor from many different countries. We left the harbor about seven p.m. There are lights on shore along the channel for miles and miles. This is a clean, beautiful ship. I sleep well with the motion. We had poached salmon and fresh raspberries for supper.

March 3rd

The water is smooth and we see many ships in the distance. Potatoes are served every day for lunch and dinner. There are many other dishes to choose from. Many of the crew are from Argentina as are the stewardesses. The officers are mostly all Norwegian.

March 10th

We are on our way to Rio. The water has been more rough the last three days and I was motion sick yesterday and the evening before. Ear patches help and now I am wearing one. There is so much food served and all good. The Norwegian officers are friendly and interesting.

Every Wednesday and Saturday at five p.m. there is a cocktail hour and Ivaran bears the cost. It is a time to socialize and get better acquainted. Officers dress in their black slacks and white shirts. I have not figured out all of their titles. One was swearing in Norwegian and I understood it and translated it. He was quite embarrassed and vowed to be more careful.

They like kumla, lutefisk, lefse and other Norse goodies we are familiar with. One of them is fond of the polka

We crossed the Equator and I can prove it!

He is never wrong about anything!

The Captain socializes with everyone.

Charles shows true interest in the ship's details.

dance. Dance is pronounced dahnse. On Sunday they serve Bloody Marys and beer on the deck at noon. The standard food Sunday noon is pizza, hamburgers and hot dogs with Norwegian beer or wine.

The Cross the Equator Party last night was fun. Each passenger received a tee shirt with the ship's name and a cap. We had to wear these to the party. Out on the deck there was a grill about five feet long and three feet wide covered with different kinds of meat. Cocktails were from 6 p.m. to 7 p.m. and food was served on the deck. We all looked the same in our tee shirts and caps. We were presented with a certificate that we had crossed the Equator. We are considered tadpoles until we have made the crossing.

The ship is rolling quite a lot and wakes me up at night. There is a man at our dinner table who I call Little Lord Fauntleroy (not to his face, of course). He is precise in his speech, never wrong about anything and gloats that he is a George Bush man. I'm reading too much but it is very hot on the deck and I don't go out there much. The ship is all air-conditioned.

Sunday - March 15th

This morning the Bloody Mary party was held on the deck from eleven to twelve noon. It was a beautiful morning. The sea was not rough and the color bright blue. Last night was the Saturday cocktail hour and dinner. After dinner, the dessert and coffee were served in the sitting room along with cognac for those who wished for it. The Captain socializes with everyone.

Charles and I were invited to Per's cabin. He is the First Engineer. He likes Charles and says Charles is the only passenger that asks intelligent questions and shows a true interest. No one enters an officer's cabin without an

invitation and even then, the officers get permission from the Captain.

This Captain is very sociable. His hobbies are doing embroidery and hardanger in his spare time. His name is Peder Sydness and his home is Bergen, Norway. He embroiders on dresses for his daughters.

The Chief Steward's name is Svend Carlsen. I'm sure every available lady who has come on this ship could cuddle up to him. He is funny without meaning to be and has a charming, heavy brogue. He is responsible for all the food, parties and keeping the passengers comfortable.

The Chief Engineer is Ernst. He, too, has a heavy brogue. He is married to an American and makes his home in Florida. He is the one who likes to do the polka dance. He is very friendly.

Thursday - March 19th

If there is in the world a more beautiful harbor than Rio de Janeiro it would be a big, big surprise. It is mountainous and very, very green. There was a tour bus that took us into the city and entertained us, compliments of Ivaran Shipping. Those with unlimited bank accounts shopped. We were among those who took the cable car to the top of Sugar Loaf Mountain. It is a place to observe for miles and miles.

We were taken to lunch at the Cococabana, a fine place by the beach. There are 160 beaches in Rio and most are public. Lunch consisted of beef, chicken, lamb and pork. Many kinds of salads. The meat was sliced at our table. We did not see the poverty that is in every city. Many live in paper boxes in the hills. Our tour guide told us the police do not even go into those areas due to danger.

SHIP'S LOG

We visit South America's largest port and do some people-watching

Our radio operator was arrested on a drug charge!

The ship sways as they load it.

Passengers and officers are quite congenial. One woman has a talent for putting down others and making caustic remarks. We try to stay away from her. She did smile at me twice. She demands attention from the Chief Steward. Later, I found out her marriage is unhappy and she has, in a round-about-way, apologized for her unhappiness.

After Rio, we were off to Santos, Brazil, the largest port in South America with ships from many countries. Here we were allowed about five hours. We took a taxi into the city along with Lou, from British Columbia. We milled around a shopping mall but did not buy anything. We settled down at a sidewalk cafe with sandwiches, beer and fruit juice and watched people.

It was an enjoyable afternoon. Lou is fine company and taught school in her earlier years. We found Newsweek (not the edition with which we are familiar) but no English newspapers. In Rio, we did find one English newspaper.

Friday - March 20

We are at sea all day. We docked at Montevideo, Uruguay in the night. Some freight was unloaded and by morning we were at sea again. Some of the crew are from here. Our radio operator is from here and planned to leave the ship here. He was arrested on a drug charge and spent the night in jail. He called the Captain to post bail but was refused in no uncertain terms. He was a handsome young man, very nice to me and liked to visit. He had sad eyes and a far-away look.

March 30, 1992 - Harbor at Buenos Aires

Horrors, it is long since I have written and there is much to tell. The ship is being loaded with containers. I hear we carry 600 of them. The ship sways as they load

SHIP'S LOG

and makes my writing barely legible. We got off the ship in Buenos Aires (B.A.) on Sunday last - eight days ago. A van took us to the Lancaster Hotel and we were there seven days. It is an old hotel but elegant in many ways. Some of the passengers complained but we were happy with the accommodations. Why complain when Ivaran paid for it all? We also got our $50.00 a day each food allowance.

A cemetery in Buenos aires for the wealthy.
Eva Peron is buried here – it's a popular tourist attraction.
(The tomb pictured here is not that of Eva Peron.)

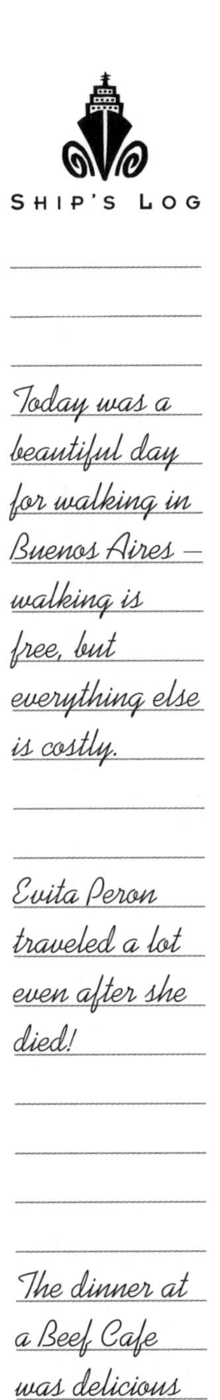

We were near the shopping part of the city but bought very little. My right foot has been hurting. Must have twisted it somehow. Had to stop at a pharmacy and get an elastic bandage to wrap it. It slowed me down. Charles bought two sweaters and I bought one, plus a pair of cheapy slacks made in the U.S.A. Thought I might need them for warmth.

It was a beautiful day for walking around at the shops. We had a slice of pizza (not as good as ours) and a Pepsi. In the hotel, a glass of orange juice costs $5.00; a can of German beer was $6.00; a small bowl of ice was $5.00; and a vodka tonic was $8.00. Charles and I walked to a beef eating place (EL CHARRO) and had a fine meal. With wine it cost $40.00.

We took a city tour on Tuesday. In a park, there grows the largest rubber tree in the world we are told. It would fill almost our whole farm yard at home. After that, we walked through the most unusual graveyard anyone can imagine. All mausoleums built right next to each other. All different kinds of stone and marble with intricate design. Evita Peron is buried there. Her body was stolen and taken to Italy but later retrieved and brought back to Argentina. Now the body is under a lot of steel and concrete. This graveyard covers about four square blocks. In these mausoleums there are stairs leading down to a small room where relatives of the dead have tea and meditation.

After this we were taken for dinner to a Beef Cafe. I could not even eat one-third of it but it was delicious. Then off to an evening musical. There was much tango dancing and enchanting Argentine music. The orchestra was eleven pieces, including a grand piano, four accordions and violins. The Bolivian Indians performed in their native dress and played string instruments, some of which they had made themselves. These are very talented

SHIP'S LOG

people and handsome. If there is ever a chance to see this show again I would go in a minute. The tango is a beautiful dance and quite suggestive. It was banned at one time.

The next day five of us took a tour to a ranch. There was a huge building, open air at the sides. On the way we saw the pampas (flat lands) where cattle grazed. This is big cattle and horse country. Beef and chicken were

Each tomb in the cemetery has its sad history. A fascinating place.

25 countries represented at fun dinner.

Rope tricks were performed by handsome Gauchos.

Iguassu Falls was impressive to Eleanor Roosevelt. and me.

A beautiful area but don't drink the water!

cooked over a huge circular coal fire. After we had eaten there was musical entertainment. There was dancing and wine and beer were flowing freely.

The M.C. announced different countries people were from and there must have been at least 25. As each country was called, those people stood up and there was much clapping and yelling. Just some of the countries were Canada, only a few Americans, Mexico, Puerto Rico, England, Sweden, Finland, France, Italy, Argentina, Brazil, Bolivia, Colombia, Chile, China, Taiwan, Australia and more.

There were youngsters from Colombia on holiday (smoking funny stuff) having fun. There was much dancing and even I danced with the Columbians. The Gauchos are extra-handsome. Each had his own color horse and all did some fine riding. They did rope tricks and showed their accuracy and skill.

We took one more tour the week we were in B.A. We flew to Iguassu Falls for an overnight thing. These are famous falls on the Brazil-Argentine border very close to Paraguay. Two rivers come together here and flow into the Platte which eventually reaches the Atlantic. When Eleanor Roosevelt saw these falls she said it made Niagara Falls look like a kitchen faucet. Iguassu is an Indian name meaning big water.

We stayed at a five-star hotel. It was refreshing to get out and take the walking paths and there were many. It was lush and green everywhere. It was five hundred miles up there and we had to be at the city airport at 5:30 a.m. The plane was a Boeing 727 and loaded to capacity. Iguassu is a tourist place but not very commercialized as yet. We ate lunch in a nearby town in Brazil. Did not dare drink the water. Signs in the airport warned about that.

SHIP'S LOG

I was afraid we were making an emergency landing.

Impatient members of our tour cause us embarrass-ment.

Some people feel tipping is a good thing.... for someone else to do!

The next day we took a long walk on a walking bridge leading right up to the falls. It was a hot day but there was a breeze which helped. The overall view was a joy to see. We do not have such a place in our country that I am aware of. Our plane left at 2:40 p.m. to fly back to B.A.

We were thirty-five minutes into the flight when there were threatening thunder heads that looked quite dangerous. The pilot dodged them as best he could but soon he was coming lower and lower, almost on top of the jungle. I was afraid we were making an emergency landing or that it was the end of us. The Captain announced what was happening but he spoke Spanish. There was no landing strip and no town.

All of a sudden a landing strip appeared, much to my relief. I had feared it was time for last rites! We found ourselves back at Iguassu. (Quite an experience) The storm was all the way across the continent. We were at the airport about one and a half hours before taking off again. We were three hours late getting back to B. A. Later that evening we had a ham and cheese sandwich at a sidewalk cafe. Back at the Iguassu airport we were given vouchers for refreshments. Two in our party were angry we did not get waited on right away. That can be embarrassing for the rest of us.

Charles had carried our bags to the van and the porter carried two other women's bags and Charles did the tipping! Some watch their money too carefully. My foot troubled me some with the walking we have been doing.

Not long left for us to be in B.A. Three of us walked down the street and enjoyed lasagna in an Italian restaurant. I had not eaten for many hours and felt faint after the meal. It was only three blocks to our hotel but we had

The first engineer likes to unwind at the cocktail parties.

Striking longshoremen make us change ports.

No great shopping, but some donkeys.

We are permitted to enter a huge Russian ship.

I rubbed cheeks with a Russian guard!

to take a cab. I went straight to bed and felt fine in the morning.

Sunday, March 29th, we were taken back to the ship. We were all happy to get back on board. The Chief Steward had a cocktail hour, dinner and coffee cake and brandy in the dining room. The first engineer gets a little high on alcohol at these parties and likes to talk. His name is Per and his brogue is severe. He is a tough Norwegian and works hard.

Monday - March 30th

Time to do laundry after all these tours and time to wash hair. We were to stop at Montevideo next but the longshoremen are on strike so we will bypass this port and go to Itaja, Brazil. The Captain wanted to leave here by 5:00 p.m. but we left much later.

Early this morning I watched the tugs pull us to the dock at Rio Grande, Brazil. Yesterday I sat on the upper deck in my swim suit but today it is cloudy and cool. All the other passengers went into town but again I prefer to stay on board. Wrote three letters to folks back home. When the shoppers came back they reported no desirable shopping and some donkeys.

Along side us at the dock is a huge Russian ship. There was a large opening in the hold. Charles and I walked over there and the guard let us walk around in the hold but would not permit us to go to the upper decks. In the hold were many small combines (Massey Ferguson, I believe) that were loaded in Rio Grande and being shipped to Morocco.

The guard was young and handsome. We exchanged cheek rubs. He spoke just a little English. Charles took our picture but the camera was loaded wrong and it did not turn out. Some of the Russian crew were fishing off

the dock. When I asked one of them if his country is Russia or the Soviet Union, he uttered Soviet Union and did not recognize that the Soviet Union was already becoming democratized.

He has traveled extensively. We only wish it had been somewhere else.

One passenger is a man of arrogance. He projects a cold attitude and I believe would never fit in the South American culture. He is not openly rude to others but simply ignores them. He is from a southern state and looks down on black people, Democrats and most who disagree with him. We discussed the ranch where we had gone on a day trip. He claimed the dancing was cheap, the food was bad and the whole thing was phony. The rest of us were not expecting a five-star restaurant and we enjoyed getting out of the city. Our relationship was cool after this episode. He has traveled extensively.

Maybe he is my boyfriend. No, says Janet.

One of the crew who does a lot of welding down below loves visiting with Charles because Charles has been a farmer and a cattleman. This man has a smiley, comical face. He comes from the Ukraine. He told me yesterday I am special! Anyway, I think maybe he is my boyfriend but Janet (another passenger) says he is hers! We laugh about that.

April 2nd, 1992

Orange juice and coffee starts my day.

Did not sleep well last night. Felt motion sick and put a patch by my ear and took aspirin. Bad dreams plagued me and I was happy to come awake and realize they were only dreams. Got up early, went to the dining room and brought freshly squeezed orange juice and coffee back to the cabin for Charles and me. This I do almost every morning.

After lunch I went to the bridge and the radio man, Jose, put a call through for me to Angela Marchi in Londrina, Brazil. We are along the coast of Brazil. Angela is

SHIP'S LOG

the wife of Marcos Marchi who stayed with our family at the farm near Sharon, ND. She and I have not met. Angela tells me they are in their harvest season and perhaps will not be able to come to Santos next Sunday and Monday while we are there. I told her, if not, we will meet in the USA sometime. The call costs $10.00.

April 7th, 1992

A couple of Romanians enjoy a visit with us.

Writing in this book is long overdue. We did dock at Santos (largest port in South America). It is fun to watch the tugs pull and push the ship to the dock. On Saturday night two of the women from our ship met a couple of Romanians from another ship and brought them aboard for a drink. I gave them cigarettes and Charles gave them caps he had brought along. They seemed to be delighted with the camaraderie.

A lesson in Brazilian history was given by Ingrid.

Sunday there was a tour planned for those who wanted to go to Sao Paulo. This was a one hour bus ride over the mountains. We were taken to a museum in beautiful lush gardens and given a lesson in Brazilian history. Our tour guide's name was Ingrid. She has a Swedish father and Brazilian mother. She is a student at Sao Paulo University majoring in marine biology. We were taken through the grounds of this university of 40,000 students. The education is free to those who can pass the entrance exams.

I get a phone call! What a shock!

Lunch was at a restaurant of too much food, as usual. I ate light. There are many potholes in the streets and the lurching of the bus made me queasy. I was sitting, eating in this restaurant in a strange foreign country in a city of 20 million with outlying districts, and I get a phone call! What a shock! I was afraid my whole family had gone over a cliff. Those in our party were stunned, too.

SHIP'S LOG

Marcos still has a twinkle in his eye.

We looked at family pictures.

The large plantation employs as many as 2,000 workers.

It was Angela Marchi from southern Brazil. She said it was not hard to find me. She had called the Ivaran Office and they told her I might be at this cafe. We made an appointment to meet at the harbor gate tomorrow at ten a.m. in Santos and go for lunch. On the way back to Santos, Charles bought for me a large bouquet of roses. These are sold at roadside outdoor displays.

Angela and Marcos came to the harbor gate at ten a.m. Angela is most attractive. Marcos' hair is gray now and he still has a twinkle in his eye. It was thrilling to see him after so many years. It would have been about 1969 when he was at the farm. We went in their car and took a ferry to an island and sat in a hotel courtyard and visited.

For lunch we had to go indoors as it was too hot to sit outside. Marcos remembers everyone he met in North Dakota and asked about everyone. We looked at family pictures. Marcos never forgets his visit to North Dakota but Angela complains he will never speak English. He wasn't very good at it either.

They insist we come back and visit them and stay a month. Angela gave to me a leather tray with intricate designs and bunches of grapes made of quartz which comes from a mine and can be different colors. Charles and Marcos talked farming and cattle. The Marchi family employ 2,000 workers at the height of the busiest season and 200 the rest of the year. These 200 workers and their families have their own village at the edge of the plantation.

They grow a variety of crops including soybeans and coffee. Cattle, too, are a part of the operation. The Marchi family provide everything for the workers including food and housing. Angela worries about her country.

Too many cannot read and write. They stay around the beaches and live on fish and fruit from the trees. They don't want work. We had to say goodbye at the harbor gate. They could not enter without proper papers. We had to promise to return.

Monday - April 13th

A gray, rainy day. We are headed northwest to the island of the Dominican Republic. It will take several days. We crossed the Equator again and had another barbeque on the deck. The weather was perfect. Any of the crew who aren't working come to the party and visit, plus the officers. One of the crew who is from the Ukraine gave me a big smack on the cheek and said, "When I look into your eyes, I want to make your life beautiful." I answered, "My life is beautiful." He was not to be put off and answered, "But, I could make it more beautiful!" Maybe he said the same to all the women. He, Dimitri, was happy to hear of our farm background.

Charles and I are walking along the harbor and we meet the Chief Engineer, Ernst. His wife lives in Florida. He has a charming brogue and tells us, "I called my vife (wife) last night." I ask, "Does she miss you, Ernst?" He says, "I don't know about dat but ve (we) have an increase in our family." I'm happy for him and, of course, the next question was, "Do you have a new baby?" "No, my vife bought a dawg!" He pronounces it dawg. "What kind of a dog is it?" "A mixed dawg." He was not happy about it. I tell him there may be a litter of puppies by the time he gets home but he sputters and says, "That will not be, his name is Joe." Ernst is very nice. He grew up in Norway.

In the port of Salvador, Brazil, the chief steward arranged a bus trip for us into the city. This appeared to be a very poor city. We went on such narrow streets and saw such poor buildings and small businesses. It is diffi-

cult to describe. There is also an area of extreme wealth. No in-between of poor and rich.

Charles saves bus passengers from the heat!

Charles and I stayed on the bus while some in our party walked a long distance to see churches. It was very hot! We were parked in a very poor area and waited for the others. Charles found a stand nearby and brought cold beer to those still on the bus. There was a very nice gift shop and jewelry shop nearby. I went to the shop and, lo and behold, the owner was from London and his wife from Ireland.

Sweet as love, black as night, an' hot as hell.

It was a surprise to find an English speaking couple in this part of the city. He invited me to have a complimentary cup of coffee. It is said in Brazil coffee is served sweet as love, black as night and hot as hell. I had an interesting chat with this couple as we delved into our backgrounds.

Leather bargains are too much to resist.

After this, we were taken to an open air mall. It did have a roof but sides open and a dirt floor. There was everything for sale you could name. Charles bought leather boots and sandals. I bought a belt and a leather cap for my grandson. All of these cost $50.00. There were many lovely handmade articles.

The Captain wants us to check out anyone in North Dakota named Sydness. He had relatives at one time in Minot. The Captain makes one more trip and then he has four months off to be with his family in Norway.

We may be relaxing but ship's work goes on.

It seems as though I could get blown into space! One of the crew is making a horrible noise by our window. He is working on the lifeboat, either repairing or removing paint for a touch up.

SHIP'S LOG

My Jewish friend grew up in Vienna and ignored good advice.

The door bell rang and she was terrified!

Ella escaped to New York and had a hard time.

April 14th - At sea somewhere north of South America

We have sailed a long distance since Salvador but have a way to go to reach the Dominican Republic. I am reading regularly but the only book of value is Charles Dickens' Great Expectations.

One of the Jewish women and I have become friends. We both make fun of ourselves. When no one else was around, she wanted to tell me about her past life. She came to my cabin and we had at least an hour or two for exchanging ideas and past events. She was born in Vienna. Her father worked in a bank. The year of 1937 Hitler was becoming worrisome and Jews were disappearing off the streets. My friend Ella was a student at Vienna University studying Psychology. Her father wanted her to leave and go to Switzerland. She was in the middle of her studies and ignored his warning.

Jews were being arrested and her father was frightened. Her door bell rang in the middle of the night and she was terrified. It was a cable from her father to leave immediately. She got one of the last four visas given to students. She had to turn in her passport to get the visa stamped in it. To be caught without a passport was the death penalty. Some of the Jews went to Israel in the underground movement. She went to Zurich, Switzerland.

Ben Gurion came to Switzerland and Ella spoke to him about escape but it was a disappointment. He was not interested in her problem.

In 1940 she came to New York. Having little money and no relatives, this was a hard time. She didn't even know the language but got a job in an ice cream store running machines, bought an English book and taught

The horror is hers always.

We both had tears in our eyes.

Chief steward Svend plans a Norwegian Night with lutefisk, of course.

Everything was a work of art!

herself the language. I don't know to whom she got married but they had two children. There was a divorce and she came eventually to Cincinnati where there were several Jewish families.

Her parents perished under Nazi rule. Her father cleaned toilets for the Nazis. It was a terrible time. Ella was poor and taught herself the stock broker business by studying. She married again and they were together twelve years before his death. He had lived in a nursing home four of those years. The horror of those years is with her always.

The other Jewish woman on the ship had lost her parents by murder. The Nazis saw to this. There is a book that has been published of an oral history of Cincinnati families. It is titled Refuge in Cincinnati by Abraham Peck. These people want their offspring to know and remember how it was. Ella says civilization is running on a very slim track and it could all happen again. We both had tears in our eyes when we spoke about this.

Svend, our chief steward, is planning a Norwegian Night tomorrow. He is including lutefisk, a favorite of Norwegians, and served with melted butter. We have had fish up to our eyeballs. It is all good. There is salmon, cod, herring, halibut, and many other kinds I cannot name.

Charles and I took a walk to the lower deck and visited with two officers who had worked in the heat all day and were sharing a bottle of wine.

April 15th, 1992

This is Norwegian Night and I'm not kidding. Every thing was artistically done, even to the liver paté and chicken paté. One of our southern friends did his best with Jack Daniels. He claims he had to use his hands to

straighten out his face this morning. Ernst walked me through the dinner line to see that I took the right stuff. There are always potatoes and another of their favorites are mashed peas and rutabaga. None of the other passengers would touch the lutefisk. After the meal, there was cake, coffee and cognac in the sitting room.

It is hot and we are approaching the Dominican Republic. We will dock there in the morning. We will go ashore for awhile into the city of Santo Domingo. Some of us had sandwiches and cold drinks in a lovely courtyard full of greenery, exotic birds and heat! This was Good Friday and most of the shops were closed. We saw the huge, old church where Columbus is buried. I bought three small straw hats for the little girls in Fargo. They cost $1.00 each. Charles bought cigars for C. T. Anderson.

When I answer a tap at the door this afternoon, Lou is there and blurts out, "The last one in the pool is a rotten egg!" I immediately get into my swimming suit and get out there. The water is tepid and don't get it in the eyes or mouth, it is salty.

The U.S. Coast Guard had a ship in this area today and a plane buzzing this ship. They wanted to know many details as to how many passengers, business of the ship and destinations. The Captain was most annoyed!

Easter Sunday - April 19, 1992

A man's body was floating in the water nearby.

This is a hot, sunny morning somewhere in the Caribean. We are all looking forward to arriving at New Orleans. Two days ago in the port of Santo Domingo there was a ship at the dock near us, bound for where I have no idea. There was a man's body floating in the water nearby. He was a stowaway who tried to enter the ship from below and was killed when the engines started.

It was a "hot" time at the deck party we hosted.

Stowaways are common. People are desperate to leave some of these countries. The ships pay a huge fine if these people are not found and returned.

Charles and I hosted the deck party this morning. We invited everybody. This takes place each Sunday from 11:00 a.m. to 12:00 noon. Bloody Marys, soft drinks and beer are served along with cheese, crackers and raw veggies. It was so hot this morning the crew really put away the beer. They were reluctant to come and help themselves so I waited on them. Charles, too, socialized and saw that they did not leave thirsty.

Jack Daniels did this fellow in from head to toe.

Each Sunday lunch, pizza, hot dogs and hamburgers are the menu. A passenger from Tennessee mixed the Bloody Marys for us. I don't know how he does it. Last night he was into the Jack Daniels to the point of needing help to remove his shoes. He is a cozy, warm fellow but his wife was ticked at him. Everyone enjoyed the Sunday morning party and Dimitri was generous with his kisses. In the afternoon I had a nap and a dip in the pool. It was a beautiful evening. Cuba is to our north and the Caymen Islands to our south.

Monday - April 20th, 1992

The Captain's farewell dinner for the passengers didn't help my waistline.

Oh! What a hot day! I washed clothes and we paid Svend for what we had bought aboard ship and for the Sunday party. That did not cost much. Lou and I found a spot on deck under a lifeboat where there was a breeze. The Captain had a farewell dinner. There was an appetizer served in a grapefruit shell, lobster thermidor and rice, lamb and vegetables and baked Alaska. All was prepared and served quite artistically. After dinner there was coffee and cognac in the sitting room. I'm not getting any thinner.

April 21st

This is our last full day at sea. It is cool today. We are packing little by little, hoping customs won't unpack it all again.

April 22nd

We docked in New Orleans this morning at 7:00 a.m. Customs came on board at 9:30 a.m. and we met in the Captain's office. Our passports were returned to us and they did not inspect any of our luggage. They only wanted to know what we had bought and its value. The Captain had made reservations for us at the Monteleon Hotel in the French Quarter. He also got our airline tickets changed to April 23rd.

The agent of Ivaran came on board and checked everyone to be sure reservations were in order. He brought a telephone message that I was to call home. This alarmed me and I had to wait a long time to get access to the phone as two women were using it a long time just prattling. By the time I got to use it, murder was uppermost in my mind but I didn't know how to get rid of the body. Anyhow, finally when I did call, there was nothing urgent. I was so relieved I cried.

Some time was spent saying goodbye to everyone. We would not see most of these folks again. It was sad but yet there was joy in heading home. A van came to the ship to take us to our hotel. It was a lovely hotel and air conditioned, one block from Bourbon Street. Charles, Lou and I had a sandwich for lunch and were going walking. It was too hot for me to walk and I stayed in the air conditioned room.

In the evening we met Lou again and walked Bourbon Street, listening to Dixie Land music in several bars. The music was so good and all the old songs were played.

SHIP'S LOG

It's wonderful to be home.

Many memories I will always cherish.

Eight months of planning is good procedure.

If you're angry go to the bridge and scream!

We gave up at midnight. Lou was flying out early for Prince George, British Columbia. I stopped at the beauty salon in the hotel and had the first professional hairdo in 60 days. What an improvement! We left the city at 3:00 p.m. The flight home was rough at times but all went well. Wonderful to be home.

There are incidents I have forgotten to write but certain impressions will stay with me. Some of them are:

1. The handsome, warm South Americans.
2. The delight of knowing the Norwegians and their charming accents.
3. The beauty of entering a port and watching the tugs pushing and pulling to get us to the dock.
4. The poverty that was so evident in many places and the sadness of it. In Sao Paulo our tour guide said there are one-half million abandoned children who live in the streets.

It took nearly eight months to plan this trip. We needed passports, visas for Brazil, cholera shots, a 10% down payment and the balance six weeks prior to the voyage and a medical certificate that we were fit to travel. There was no doctor aboard. All of the above were required by certain dates prior to sailing.

We each paid $6,000.00 for this trip. This amounted to slightly over $100.00 per day; included was the ride, all meals, some city tours and shows, cabin upkeep and fun social gatherings. We felt the cost was not extravagant.

Just two more afterthoughts:

Kjetil is the young Norwegian electrician and gave me a little advice. He said, "When you get angry on the ship, go to the bridge, look out at the water and scream!"

SHIP'S LOG

Where will our next trip take us?

A black curly-haired young crew member from Santiago, Chile, approached Charles one evening and suggested they go into the city and find a couple of pretty young girls. He said it would not be difficult to do this. Charles replied, "But I have a wife!" Young Victor said, "That doesn't matter, leave her on board!" We had a good laugh over this.

Where will we go on our next trip? Charles says we can plan it later this summer. He thinks we can decide on a Sunday and leave the following day. We shall see.

CHAPTER II

Tragic Events

June 8, 1992

The last picture taken of Charles and Frances Flynn.
Aboard the MV Santa Fe somewhere in the Gulf of Mexico.
April, 1992.

SHIP'S LOG

A goodbye kiss.

I felt there must be bad news.

We could barely speak.

Chapter II

June 8, 1992

It is difficult to write this chapter but it must be done. Charles and I have been home from our trip 38 days. We were already talking about our next trip. Where and when. I awakened at 5 a.m. this day because I had registered for a humanities class at Mayville State University. This class met at 7:00 a.m. and I looked forward to it. I gave Charles a smack on the forehead and we would meet at dinner. He was going to Eckelson to check the farm. We never met again.

About 11:00 a.m. Jim Flynn called to say Charles had collapsed at the farm and was being taken to the Jamestown Hospital. He said he would call when there was news. He didn't call. He didn't call. He didn't call. By this time, I felt there must be bad news. There was. About one or two o'clock the call came that Charles was dead. I'm not able to describe my feelings.

I walked the floor for awhile. Realizing that I had to do something, I called my daughter-in-law Gay. She and I and Rachel and Sonia drove to Valley City to see Jim. We could barely speak. Charles' body was being taken to Fargo for an autopsy. There were arrangements to be made but not this day. After making a few plans, we drove back home. In a paper sack in the back seat were Charles' clothes. When Rachel and Sonia looked in the bag, silence in the back seat was deafening. None of us knew how to carry on any conversation. Family members

Ship's Log

Many friends and relatives attended.

I was told it would take three years for the pain to ease.

had to be called, a difficult thing that I could not do. Thanks to Gay who seemed more composed and rational. My sons in Alaska were making plans to come home. If the planes flew as scheduled, they would be here. They did come. Now, Charles' burial clothes must be chosen and a coffin chosen. I had help from others and had I not been in a state of insensibility, it would not have been done properly. Oh! we got through the service and the burial at Sacred Heart Church in Sanborn. Many friends and relatives attended. Charles was highly regarded by so many. He was loved by my family and his brother Jim's family.

The day after the funeral some of Jim's family came to the farm. Food was brought by neighbors and friends. The Eastern Star chapter from Finley provided us with a meal you could get your teeth into. We are all grateful for the visits and sympathetic words. They were all sincere and welcomed.

It wasn't long before my family had to return to their jobs. I spent my time writing thank you notes. A lot of the memorial money was given to the Shrine Children's Burn Center in Cincinnati. This hospital has helped a young Flynn child who was burned tragically. It took some time to write 400 thank you notes but it was a part of the healing process. A very elderly French woman I would meet on a ship told me it would take three years for the pain to ease. She could not speak English but we had an interpreter. She is a wise woman.

It has been said of Charles that he communicated with young people. True. One letter I received thanked me for bringing him to this community. The dearest letter came from a most unlikely source. I cannot write the details but Charles had encouraged this person when she fought cancer and struggled through a divorce. This, I

SHIP'S LOG

A love story that continued for twenty wonderful years.

was not aware of. He had even given her a real Christmas tree instead of a fake. The letter was precious.

Charles and I cared for each other deeply. Being married to him was like living on the edge. What a wonderful time that continued twenty years. Many face adversity and death. I do not relate this story to gain sympathy. I tell it mostly to tell a love story.

CHAPTER III

The MV Santa Fe Beckons Again

October 1992

—

December 1992

MV SANTA FE

Steaming ahead. This ship does about 18 to 19 knots per hour.
The service is five-star.

SHIP'S LOG

A free ticket was offered as an incentive.

You cannot board without a passport.

I was off to far off places... alone!

No one sat next to me.

Chapter III

Late summer of 1992

Ivaran shipping offered me a free airline ticket to Rio de Janeiro or to London if I wanted to sail again on the Santa Fe. I was very apprehensive traveling to either of these places not knowing anyone and no one to meet me. It was easier to go to London where language should not be a problem. It took a week to prepare after most of the plans were completed.

I needed a doctor's certificate showing no health problems of an alarming nature but did need a three month supply of blood pressure pills and ear patches for motion sickness. A visa was required for Brazil plus plane tickets, ship tickets and a host of other details. You cannot board without a passport.

October 14th, 1992

Jim Flynn came to the farm to get me and I was on my way to far off places alone. From the Fargo airport to Minneapolis I was on a very small plane that I could not stand up in. At Minneapolis I had to gather my carry-on bag and get to the main terminal on a shuttle bus to where overseas flights were loading.

My ticket and passport were inspected at the desk and my passport was checked again when I boarded the plane. This was on an almost eight-hour flight all night. Dinner was served and cocktails were free. No one sat next to me and I could put my feet up.

SHIP'S LOG

They all knew where they were going except me.

A taxi ride would be too expensive.

Lord Nelson is one of my heroes.

The woman in front of me is from Idaho. She is 82 years old and traveling to Spain alone. She has been many places and looks much younger than 82. The fellow across from me is from Denmark and knows only two English words...Kansas City. He drank beer all night and smoked constantly. Flying over England at sunrise was beautiful. It looked green and well-groomed.

Deplaning was bedlam. People everywhere. They all knew where they were going except me and I couldn't spot an information desk. I followed the crowd, got on an airport tram, not even knowing where I would end up. Then I got into a long line and got checked into the country. From there it was to pick up luggage and try to find a taxi.

The information people told me it would cost 100 pounds to take a taxi to where I wanted to go. By my calculations, that was $150.00 or more. I then got instructions to take the train. After buying the train ticket I boarded a train from the airport to Victoria Station in London. All this time, I was wheeling luggage which was no small feat. The train was first class, clean, and fast.

From Victoria Station I had to take a taxi to Fenchurch Street Station to board another train. The taxi driver was a friendly, polite fellow and took me by Buckingham Palace and Trafalgar Square. Lord Nelson is one of my heroes and I was happy to see that. He pointed out interesting sights and told me he was born during the bombing of London. At that dangerous time pregnant women were taken out of London to rural country estates.

At Fenchurch Station I had to get a train to Grays which is very near the hotel where I had a reservation. At Grays, I got another taxi to take me to the hotel which

SHIP'S LOG

The dining room is lovely and the old fashioned service is unbelievable.

British television is so funny

"She was a naughty girl."

was about four miles away. One of the train men helped me across a rather busy street to a cab stand. People have been dear and helpful. As far as hotels go, I didn't know what to expect but was delightfully surprised to find an old fashioned hotel with 22 rooms that looked like a country estate mansion. The grounds are beautifully landscaped.

The taxi driver thinks I am Canadian. He was annoyed that I still had American money but he got his due and then some. The dining room of this hotel is lovely with a huge fireplace and the tables are adorned with white tablecloths and napkins. Meals are served only at certain hours. I did not go down for breakfast and at lunch asked for a roll and a glass of wine. The manager brought it to my room. Can you imagine that happening in the U.S.?

October 16th, 1992

There was quite a party at this hotel in the eve. It was a dinner dance for a certain group. The music came from compact discs and was a lot of Glenn Miller. British television is so funny. Their humorists speak correctly but say almost anything in a delicate way. Their satire dwells a lot on American politics. They even had a hilarious skit of Hillary and Barbara Bush baking cookies. They poke fun at everyone and everything. The second debate between Bush, Clinton and Perot was shown by the BBC at 2:00 a.m. and I got up and watched. The BBC says Bush did nothing to enhance his chances and Perot was not effective.

October 17th, 1992

The cab driver who took me by Buckingham Palace says, "Fergie deserves everything that has happened to her. She was a naughty girl." The driver who brought me

SHIP'S LOG

Unemployment dominates the news.

The steering wheels are all on the wrong side.

Old friends greet me as I board the ship.

Norwegians make good beer.

to this hotel told me, "You did a bloody good job to find this place." American dollars are not so valuable. They are accepting my travel checks but it is an unequal exchange. The people here think my accent is Canadian. I tell them I have no accent. They are the ones who have an accent! They smile and raise their eyebrows.

The big problem in England at this time is the closing of the coal pits. The unemployment dominates the news. Thirty thousand men are out of work because of coal.

I call each day a Liverpool telephone number and talk to someone who knows when the Santa Fe will dock near here. He tells me I can board October 18th in the a.m. I leave the hotel and take a taxi to the dock (Berth 43). There is a woman taxi driver and, of course, the steering wheels are all on the wrong side. She takes me to berth 43 and there is the Santa Fe. How glad I am to see it!

When I come up the gang plank the first person I see is Dimitri. He looks at me, his mouth drops open and he utters, "Jesus Christ!" about three times. I say, "It is me, Dimitri, not Jesus Christ." He is so sad to hear of Charles' death and has tears in his eyes. He carries up my luggage and we see the Captain - Peder Sydness. I get choked up and can hardly speak. We are happy to see each other and I am pleased he is the Captain this trip. The Chief Steward is Ron Andreason and we have met in the past trip. He brings me ice, water and brandy. This has been a tense time for me in a strange country.

At 12:00 noon the fare is still hot dogs, pizza or hamburgers and Norwegian beer. This is the Sunday noon menu. Norwegians make good beer. At lunch I meet Per (1st engineer), Kjetil (electrician), and Joe (radio operator). Ernst (chief engineer) is boarding at Antwerp. I

SHIP'S LOG

Today is my wedding anniversary – memories flood my mind.

I am the only American aboard.

The food and service is five-star.

know all these officers and we have warm feelings for each other. It is almost like coming home. Containers are being loaded out here and we sail at 1400 hours from Tilbury, England. Our first stops are Hamburg, Germany and Bremen, Germany.

October 19th, 1992

Today is my wedding anniversary. Charles Flynn and I were married 18 years ago this day. Memories flood my mind. The weather is gray and rainy here in the channel. We will reach Hamburg tonight. Containers were loaded all night and we sailed early in the morning. There was no chance for a tour into the city. We are on our way to Bremen. The weather is sunny and cool. As we entered the harbor, the pilot came aboard and guided us to the dock.

The pilot that took us out of Hamburg is getting off here. We had a good chat and drink together. He speaks many languages and knows a lot of history. There is a woman aboard who works for Ivaran out of Oslo. She was once a radio operator on the ships and would love to do that again but has a 14-year-old daughter and is divorced. She leaves the ship at Antwerp. We had an interesting visit. I am the only American on board. How about that?

We are sailing in the channel again headed for Antwerp. These officers do not like this European run. Everything costs too much in Europe. They like to dock in Houston or New Orleans. The Chief Steward tells me we gather for happy hour at five o'clock. Present were the Captain, Chief Steward, the woman from Oslo and myself. The Captain says we have a party Saturday night. For evening dinner we had filet mignon. The food and service, in my judgement, is five-star.

I get almost no news of home.

The music is not pleasing to me.

"There will be blue birds over the White Cliffs of Dover..."

Fresh flowers and great food.

October 22nd, 1992

In the harbor at Antwerp there are ships everywhere. The one in the berth behind us we think is Italian.

These officers work four months followed by four months vacation. Before the German pilot left the ship, he gave me a Time Magazine dated October. I get almost no news of home.

The Captain spends his four-month vacation constructing a home near a small fjord. It will be his retirement home. I ask the officers to bring me an American newspaper if they go into Antwerp. They are amused by my interest in the World Series. A short wave radio would be a good thing to have but difficult to carry. In my cabin I can get the BBC until we are out of range. Also the Voice of America and some African stations. The music is not pleasing to me.

Friday - October 23rd

We left Antwerp Harbor this morning about 5:00 a.m. We are now sailing through Dover Straight and I can see the White Cliffs that became popular in a song. Tomorrow we will sail by Spain. The Captain says it will get hot when we reach the Canary Islands off the African Coast. There are many ships in the English Channel.

So far, we have been fed lamb chops, baked chicken, meatloaf, filet mignon and pork roast. All of that, plus the trimmings. There is always soup, salad if we want it, the entree and dessert. Coffee is served with dessert. Someone went shopping in Antwerp and brought fresh flowers that look like miniature daisies. They are deep rose with yellow centers.

I learned tonight that this ship may not come back to Tilbury, England but will go to New Orleans in the Gulf. I will like that a lot.

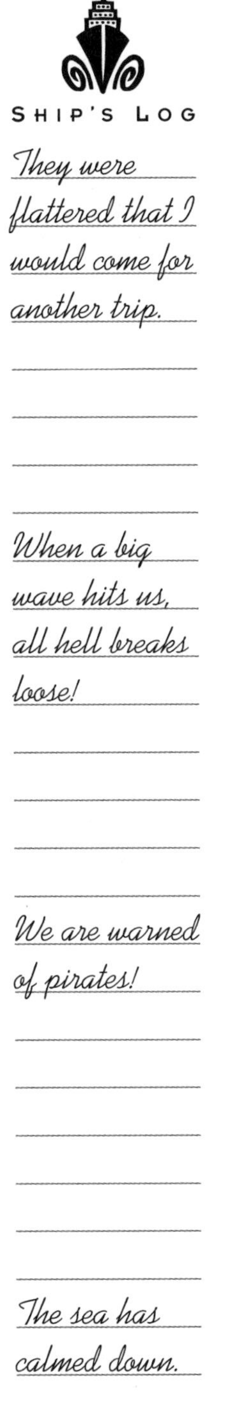

Tonight there was a happy hour and a fine dinner with socializing in the living room. Per invited two of us to his cabin for beer or a soft drink. Since Charles and I had done this last trip, I accepted. Per mostly wanted to talk about Charles and the high regard the officers had for him. Also, that the officers were pleased and flattered that I would come again for another trip.

Sunday - October 25th

This ship is rolling and rocking and pitching. The water is very choppy. The Captain says it is a huge swell coming down from the North Atlantic and we will have to bear it for two more days.

We are off the coast of Spain. Books fell off the shelves, many glasses broke in the bar and all the flower bouquets tipped over. When a big wave hits us, all hell breaks loose! While I was in bed, an apple flew off the dresser and hit me in the head.

October 26th, 1992

We are still rolling and pitching. Our next port is Rio de Janeiro and the Captain says he will not enter or leave this port in the dark. There are pirates lurking in the inlets ready to board the ships that come or go. They steal money and valuables. The sea has calmed down, making it restful and easy for a nap.

October 27th, 1992

We passed the Canary Islands in the night. That is where wealthy northern Europeans go to vacation. We are somewhere west of Africa. I thought we had a rough ride in the night but no one else seemed to think so.

October 28th, 1992

The water is smooth. The evening dinner was Norwegian food. Kumla was served. It was prepared with a

SHIP'S LOG

slice of salt pork in it and made of wheat flour. Also, yellow split pea soup and sliced cooked rutabaga. No lute fish this time.

There is a male passenger from Newcastle, England who does not want to go to New Orleans on this ship. He plans to get a different ship in Santos, Brazil and sail back to England. These plans were later changed.

October 29th, 1992

This day I helped the Newcastle passenger do his laundry. He knows nothing about washing clothes. He is 73 years old and came from Holland originally. He was in the Dutch Navy in World War II. He came to England, married and he's lived there ever since. Every single meal he says, "You can't make proper tea without biling (boiling) water." He is exact about his tea and thinks they don't know how to make it properly.

I teach him about laundry and he advises me on proper tea making.

October 30th

At 5:00 p.m. the Captain, Chief Steward, Chief Engineer, the English passenger and myself had a drink and talked about our families, retirement, our countries and many subjects.

October 31st

We are about smack dab at the equator so tonight there is a barbecue on the deck. That is a social time for everyone. All the electricity on the ship went off, causing much apprehension but it did not stay off long. I was a bit homesick this afternoon but must get over it since I am thousands of miles from home.

Crossing the Equator makes me a bit homesick.

Sunday - November 1st

I thought we had passed the Equator in the night but it is today at 5:30 p.m. At this time, some of us gathered in the sitting room. When the dials got to zero, the ship's

SHIP'S LOG

We can see the coast of Brazil.

They have everything there including the galley sink.

A dog boards our tree-less ship.

Just in case – a life boat drill.

horn was tooted, we all touched glasses to observe the special event. In the forenoon I hosted a Bloody Mary party on the deck. It was quite windy and the water in the pool sloshed back and forth soaking us. It was decided to drain the pool for this day.

Monday - November 2nd

Today we can sometimes see the coast of Brazil. We passed by an island where long ago political prisoners were held. Much cruelty occurred there. Now it is a sanctuary for birds and wildlife.

Tuesday - November 3rd, 1992

Today is Election Day in the U.S.A. The Voice of America reports Bush claims he is going to pull off the upset of the 20th century. We shall see. I had a grand tour of the galley today. There is a walk-in cooler just for fish and another for meat. Also a walk-in for fresh fruit and vegetables and another for liquor. All the ovens and sinks are stainless steel. There is also a hospital room. There is no doctor aboard but the Chief Mate has much knowledge of first aid and can even do some surgery procedures. There is another closet for medicine.

When we dock at Santos there are two women boarding. The Captain is not happy. One of the women is important in government and has a dog! What fun that will be. There are no trees or bushes on board. I volunteered to walk the dog and the Captain groaned.

November 4th, 1992

We had a life boat drill today. Quickly we donned life jackets and I was assigned to the life boat on port side. There was a social hour in the evening and the Captain had received election results by telex. Clinton beat Bush by a wide margin. Not much comment from the Norwegians.

Sometimes even motion sickness medicine is not enough.

November 5th, 1992

Thank God and the medical community for motion sickness medicine! All of a sudden the wind came up and the sea is very angry. You cannot walk now without holding on to something. We are three hours away from the dock at Rio. I have become sick even with the medicine. A cold front came up the Brazilian coast from the south. I ate bread, butter and tea for supper and went to bed. We are not going into Rio for a tour. When a wave hits us, it sounds like a gunshot.

Laura is a lovely young woman both inside and out.

November 6th, 1992

We are approaching the port of Santos. There are many ships waiting to dock. We may have to anchor in the harbor a long time waiting our turn. I just went to the dining room to get a glass of juice and I met Laura. She was a stewardess last trip and just boarded in Rio. She is a lovely young woman both inside and out. After the last trip I wrote a letter thanking everyone for a fine time and good service. She said the Captain photocopied it and gave each one a copy.

Two interesting women board at Rio.

November 7th, 1992

This is the day two women passengers boarded at Rio. They are going to Buenos Aires. One is a very elderly woman who speaks only French. She travels to Argentina from France to get away from the cold. The other woman is Brazilian but has lived many places in the world as her husband is an ambassador and they live at the present time in Portugal. She is an interesting person and we have had several talks. She is going to Buenos Aires to visit her grown children. She has lived in Thailand and Tokyo, Japan and is shortly moving to France.

The happy hour was rather strange. One group was speaking Norwegian, one group Portuguese, one group

Spanish and some of us English. The French woman chattered in French and the Captain pretended he understood but I doubt if he did. It was a strange party.

November 8th, 1992

Any excuse for a party is all that's needed.

We had a Captain's dinner as a farewell party for the Englishman who planned to leave the ship. There was a whole baked salmon, lutefisk, tenderloins and chicken, all for one meal plus many salads and vegetables. These Norwegians love parties and any excuse for one gets a party going. There must have been fifteen kinds of brandy offered after dinner. There was fun camaraderie.

November 9th, 1992

It seems our ship has priority for docking.

I had taken off my ear patch but it was a mistake. Awhile after applying one I slept a long time. We are in the La Platta river, entering the harbor of Buenos Aires. There are 12 ships I see waiting to enter and here we go straight in. Does Ivaran have priority? It does seem so.

November 10th, 1992

We are treated to a fine evening in Buenos Aires..

There is a big reception on board tonight for agents from the Ivaran office in Buenos Aires. There will be an elaborate dinner served and much liquor will flow. The Englishman never did leave the ship at Santos. He decided to proceed on to New Orleans. Since the passengers were not to attend the reception, a van and a tour guide came and took us for a tour of the city, dinner at a fine restaurant and a stage show with fine music and tango dancing.

A handsome gentleman startled me with his question.

As I sit down I see next to me a handsome gentleman very, very well-dressed. He spoke English and began a conversation. He was intrigued by news of the U.S.A. and wanted to chat. Finally, he leans over and says, "I suppose I had better not touch your leg!" My eyebrows went up and my teeth, which are permanently anchored, almost fell out. The only answer I could come up with

SHIP'S LOG

Obviously, the briberous party was not enough.

Ernst said he will never, never, never forget Charles.

We hired a tour guide and enjoyed seeing a beautiful city.

was, "You might be disappointed." Not too romantic, was it? After the show has gone on for awhile he is introduced from the stage as the Ambassador from Columbia to Argentina! We make a toast to North Dakota.

The agents who came on the ship for the reception were each given a bottle of whiskey and a carton of cigarettes. The Captain says they complain if it isn't their brand. The agents inspect and delve into everything and fine the ship $2000.00 for some sort of list they were given that they claim was not complete. Another group of inspectors called the black guards (not Negroes) came aboard and went through the crew's quarters with a fine tooth comb looking for drugs. If they find one crumb they tear the ship apart, even taking paneling off the walls. Since the ship is still intact they must not have found any.

November 11th, 1992

I slept late today after staying up late. Some of us socialized in the bar until a late hour. Ernst wanted to talk about Charles and said he will never forget Charles. Never, Never, Never! Today I met Olga Lilletvedt. She is an Argentine and was a stewardess last trip. Her husband, Svend, is a chief steward on another ship, the Americana. They were married in Norway and she showed me wedding pictures. We were happy to see each other.

November 12th, 1992

We arrived in the Port of Montevideo, Uruguay, this morning. Cornelus, the English passenger, and I hired a tour guide and each paid $30.00 to tour the city. There are beautiful parks and homes in this city of one and a half million. There are two shopping malls and we nosed around one of them and had coffee. As I stepped into the elevator the electricity went off, but thank God it came on again in a short time. We sailed again at 1:00 p.m.

November 13th, 1992

We are in the port of Rio Grande, Brazil but do not get off the ship here. We are on our way to Itaja.

November 14th, 1992

We are in the harbor of Itaja but no one will load or unload freight since it is the weekend. These stevedores do as they please. We just sit in the port.

November 15th, 1992

We are in Itaja. I'm told I can make a phone call here but I must go into the city to do it. The ship phone is for calls from out at sea. An agent from the Ivaran office takes me into the city. He is a Brazilian and speaks Spanish, Portuguese, Italian, English and Russian. I wish to call Angela Marchi who lives in southern Brazil and tell her they must not come to Santos to meet me.

We have no idea when we can dock at Santos. Always, there are strikes there. It is called a slowdown strike and the workers might load two containers an hour. Angela is not home and we leave a message.

This day a trip to shore was planned for us to a German town about one hour away. It is a lovely town settled by a German named Blumanau and the town is named for him. We had lunch high in the hills and ate German food. The view was spectacular and it was hot!

Our tour guide came from Canada and manages a children's day care where 80 youngsters come each day as their parents work. She was an interesting woman and misses not being able to buy peanut butter in that town. She has a permanent visa to Brazil allowing her to work there. She turns her salary back to the center and lives quite humbly on her tour guide income.

SHIP'S LOG

Another low work strike in Santos harbor.

All the ships in the harbor are rolling and pitching.

Not that damn funny, I told them.

Monday - November 16th, 1992

Today the stevedores are willing to work and freight is being loaded. We leave the harbor about 4:00 p.m. for Santos which is 14 hours away.

November 17th, 1992

We are in Santos harbor but not at the dock. There is another low work strike. There are over 30 ships in the harbor waiting to dock. The water is calm. The Captain tells me some of our containers carry cheese and some that go to the U.S. contain bath towels and T-shirts. There is little trade between Norway and the U.S.A. The U.S. believes Norway does too much whaling in the north Atlantic. The environmentalists have much influence about trade. The Captain tells me there are many whales in the north and it is the south Atlantic where the whaling is overdone.

Wednesday - November 18th, 1992

What a day this is! The sea has become full of swells from bad weather east of here. This day many more glasses are broken and dishes fly off into space and crash. This goes on for 24 hours and every one is weary of it. The stewardesses are sick and so am I. I used another ear patch but it took five to six hours before it did any good. All the ships in the harbor are rolling and pitching. I did eat a little dinner and the Chief Steward insists he walk ahead of me down the stairs to my cabin.

Some of the officers stood around and watched, making fun that I would fall on top of the Chief Steward. Not that damn funny! Many passengers have fallen and broken limbs. I tell the officers who are making smart remarks to go to bed and stay out of trouble. Many had severe headaches which are another symptom of motion sickness.

SHIP'S LOG

That's a lot of fuel.

The Russian ship is fined for a fuel spill

The lights of Santos were brilliant.

We survived a wild ride though Rio..

November 19th, 1992

We are still in the harbor but the sea is smooth and all of us feel better. I walk the lower deck and see a lot of beauty looking at all the ships. The first thing we do at the dock is take on about 200,000 gallons of fuel. That takes about five hours.

Friday - November 20th, 1992

We did not get to the dock today either. It is reported we will be allowed to dock at 6:00 a.m.

Saturday - November 21st, 1992

So now we are at the dock. It is so hot even the stewardesses did not go into the city. The Captain went to see a doctor about his ulcer. The Chief Steward went into the city. This is his home and he got to see his wife and child. There is a huge Russian ship next to us. They spilled a lot of fuel in the harbor and the Port Authority is fining them two million dollars! Of course, they don't have the money so the ship is under arrest and they cannot leave the harbor. The ship may be confiscated. Leaving the port this night was a beautiful sight. There was lightening in the mountains. The tugs pulled us away from the dock and we are on our way to Rio. The city and harbor lights were brilliant.

Sunday - November 22nd, 1992

We sailed into the harbor of Rio at 9:00 a.m. It was spectacular! I stood on the highest deck for one and one-half hours. The pilot boarded to take us in. It got too hot for me and I had to retreat to air-conditioning. At 1:00 p.m. a van was hired for us to go to Sugar Loaf Mountain. I have never had a more dangerous ride in my life.

The driver should enter the Indy 500. He wouldn't need practice. He drove 60 miles an hour across the city. No slow down for traffic lights, turns or lane changes. At

It would have taken a month to sort out our bodies!

intersections the largest vehicle has the right of way. Stop lights mean nothing. They are only a decoration. All the windows of the van were wide open and my hair stood on end. For more than one reason!

It was over 90 F. There were five Norwegians, two Brazilians, one man from England and myself. If we had an accident it would have taken a month to sort us out. I wondered how long it would take to ship my body back to the U.S.

Nevertheless, we were all in a jolly, good mood.

It was fun and I wouldn't have liked to miss it. We were all in a jolly, good mood and didn't worry about anything. The gang plank was going up at 3:00 p.m. and we made it back only five minutes late. The fellow from England said he had never paid anyone before to kill him. Everybody has to go sometime!

Monday - November 23, 1992

Sailing all day. It is Barbados next and that is eight days from now. I do not handle heat very well and it makes me listless. I do some walking to keep from becoming a lump.

When sailing, I do some walking and a lot of thinking.

Tuesday - November 24, 1992

I am spending too much time worrying about what is happening at home. There has been no mail for a long time. In my mind, I see Charles a lot. This is a time to grieve but also to clear cob webs from my mind. If there is anything to gossip about it spreads as fast as fire on the ship. I am being quite careful to avoid any cause of it. I talk of my family and they are all eager to hear it.

Wednesday - November 25th, 1992

A most beautiful day at sea.

This morning I took a walk on the lowest deck. It could not be a more beautiful day. The sun shone and the water was reasonably calm. All of a sudden a big wave

from nowhere washed over me. Water soaked my glasses, my mouth and my clothes. I stood on the upper deck to drip dry. Salt water doesn't taste good. The officers just laugh and make fun of me but tell me it can be dangerous walking there. The Captain says, "I hope you learned a lesson!"

Thursday - November 26, 1992 - Thanksgiving Day

The morning is fine. I don't need an ear patch but in the afternoon it all began again. Is this getting to be a habit? At five o'clock I was going to the sitting room to tell that I could not partake of the social hour. I look wilted and bedraggled. Alas! A fine turkey dinner has been prepared in my honor. I dared not back away from the preparations.

It should have been a dress up meal but now it was too late. I stayed to socialize, wearing my old washed out white shorts. A complete gourmet meal was served but eating was not what turned me on. I took a bit of each kind of food and scattered the rest around my plate. Served was a smoked salmon cocktail, turkey, chicken and vegetables. The Chief Steward brought a bowl of dressing made especially for me. I didn't dare but thank him and eat some of it. I nearly fainted it was so awful and could have lost all the dinner I had eaten. I believe my guardian angel helped me through the moment. The dressing, as far as I could tell, was bread, peas and a lot of garlic. I stayed for the coffee and brandy after dinner and shall always remember this Thanksgiving Day.

One of the stewardesses and I have become friends. Her name is Fabiana and she is 26 years old. She is Argentine and speaks very little English but we communicate quite well. She is very pretty and does not know it. We have many laughs poking fun at ourselves. She tells me

Everyone but the Captain relaxes and enjoys the party on deck.

We enjoy the beauty of Barbados.

Lots of tourists, sugar cane and rum.

she and the other stewardess go to the crew's lounge on the lower deck and dance. The Mess Boy dances, too. She tells me the music is hot!

Saturday - November 28th, 1992

We are crossing the Equator again, going north, so there is another barbecue on the deck. There is a calm sea and only a slight breeze. Pork, beef, chicken and sausage are only a part of the menu. Everyone relaxes. The Captain is suffering from what is thought to be an ulcer and is taking a lot of medicine. He will have an x-ray in Barbados.

Sunday - November 29th, 1992

The sea is rough again today. I don't go for meals but subsist on tea and toast.

November 30th, 1992

This day we sail into the harbor of Barbados. I see beauty all around me and it is hot. The water is sea green and calm. The stewardesses head for the beach. Later in the day many of the officers go into the city to eat. The city is Bridgetown and has a strong English flavor.

I tease the Chief Steward about how late they return to the ship and he replies, "We was good boys last night. Back by midnight."

There was a huge cruise ship that docked today. It is a British ship but flies a Monravia Liberian flag. The Englishman, Cornelus, and I hired a taxi and took a tour of the island. The biggest industry here is tourism and sugar cane. Unemployment is 22%. There are smaller industries, too. Here we load a lot of rum to take to Mexico. Mexicans are fond of Barbados Rum.

SHIP'S LOG

Captain plans to start living again.

We share wishes, dreams and troubles at the happy hour.

We see everything from whales to flying fish.

The fellows thought my outfit was beautiful.

December 1st, 1992

We leave the harbor about 2:00 p.m. The stewardesses are out in their short shorts yelling at the guys in the tugs. The water is clear and emerald green. The Captain found out he does not have an ulcer but acid forms and causes pain. He says now he plans to start living again. Barbados is almost 100% black. Wealthy white people come here to retire.

December 4th, 1992

The last days of sailing have been without incident. We meet for the five o'clock happy hour and get to know each other's wishes and dreams and troubles. The Captain is so wishing to go home for Christmas to Bergen, Norway. The others are getting homesick, too. After we dock in Houston they sail south again and will be at sea somewhere off the coast of Rio.

They do not want to be ashore during the holiday. It is too lonesome in the cities. Joe, the radio man, says he would leave the ship in a minute if there were any jobs in his country of Uruguay. He has three young children and is missing them. We show each other pictures.

There were two whales on the starboard side a few days ago. Two porpoises followed the ship quite a distance. We see schools of flying fish, too.

December 5th, 1992

This day the Captain decided to have his farewell dinner. For this we dress a little better so I wore my old black skirt and a black and gold blouse. Imagine! the fellows thought it beautiful. The bar opened at 5 p.m. with many present. The Captain has brought his tapes of Straus, Montavani and other good music. There is much banter.

SHIP'S LOG

Dinner is served at 6:00 p.m. It began with a seafood cocktail of shrimp and smoked salmon. It was done very artistically. The entree was smoked pork loin, baked potato and vegetables. The lights were lowered and the stewardesses entered with a flaming dessert of Baked Alaska. It was delicious. That is ice cream on a crust and browned egg white. Wine was served with dinner and coffee and brandy later.

Everyone let their hair down and had a good time.

Everyone let their hair down and all seemed to have a good time. Ernst and I even had a dance to some American music. I left the party about 10:00 p.m. The guys stayed up until all hours. Fabiana says she will miss me when I leave the ship at Houston. She has a great sense of humor.

I will be the last registered passenger on the Santa Fe. The company is trying to sell this ship and is asking six million for it. The officers say the company may get five million. Thailand shows interest in purchasing it.

Another trip? We'll see later.

The officers are expecting me to come on another voyage when the new ships are built. Two are being built in Germany. They, too, will carry 12 passengers and the word is they will sail out of New York. I have not promised anything.

December 6, 1992

A telephone call home is a big thrill for me.

The big thrill of the day was calling home from out at sea. I go to the radio room and Joe pushes many buttons to activate the call. "Santa Fe calling, Santa Fe calling" and he gives the ship's numbers. This is done with AT & T. My daughter answers and tells me everyone is fine. I hear my grand daughter Laura in the background. Joe also had to give AT & T our position. Marcia and I talk three minutes and the charge is $15.00.

We walk into Vera Cruz, Mexico to shop.

Persistent merchants are not easily discouraged.

Colorful gauchos are interesting to watch.

The streets were very clean.

Monday - December 7th, 1992

We are in Vera Cruz, Mexico. We are within walking distance of the shops and the Plaza. The Chief Steward and I have decided to walk into town after dinner. He cannot get away during the day. He speaks Spanish which helps a lot. He will not allow me to carry my purse and puts my money in his inside pocket. He wants to buy a doll for his little daughter and a gift for his wife. I want some small items to bring home to the girls. It is fun to see the wares for sale. Plenty of junk.

We walk to the large walking Plaza. There are palm trees, musical combos, eating places and booths selling soft drinks and beer. There are chairs and tables where we can sit and watch people. A bottle of beer costs $1.00. Many are trying to sell their wares or take our picture for a price. They are selling woven bags, purses, jewelry, cigars, shirts, jackets and much more.

We are harassed to buy. They are not easily discouraged. We see Ernst and Per at another table drinking a beer. They look weary and have been up since 3:00 a.m. this morning.

Ron bought a straw hat and looked so funny in it. Some gauchos were dressed in red or pink suits with many imbedded jewels. Their huge sombreros matched their suits and they carried pistols. This is all so different that it greatly interests me. We were to return to the ship at 11:00 p.m. We sail at midnight.

When we got back to the ship at 10:30 p.m. the crew were already taking off the guide ropes from the gang plank. We made it in time. The buildings in Vera Cruz are designed by Spanish builders and the streets we saw are very clean. We sailed on time.

SHIP'S LOG

Old salts like me don't get sea sick.

Cornelus tells about his service in the Dutch Navy and some terrible disasters.

Tuesday - December 8th, 1992

We are docked at a small Mexican port near Tampico. There was no need to go ashore here. We arrived here at 3:00 p.m. and were to leave at midnight but did not get away until 1:30 a.m. when the pilot guided us out of the harbor.

Wednesday - December 9th, 1992

There are big swells in the Gulf today but I no longer get sick. I'm as tough as an old salt now. This trip is rapidly coming to a close. There have been fun times and joyful times.

I must write a little about Cornelus, the man from Newcastle. He has lived in England since World War II. He was born in Holland and at the age of 17 joined the Dutch Navy about the year 1937. It was a six-year commitment. He spent four years on a submarine and six years on a battleship. When World War II broke out he was in the Indian Ocean and immediately he was in the navy for the duration.

The battleship was the newest, most modern, state-of-the-art ship in the world. It was the pride of the Dutch Navy. When it was finished being built it was taken out in very rough waters to see how it would perform. All the young sailors were called on deck and one was missing. Man Overboard! They searched and searched many hours but never did find him. That was Disaster Number One. A few days later there was an accident with the guns. Two seamen had their arms blown off in this accident. It was a sad thing for all the sailors aboard. This was Disaster Number Two.

Next, when a plane that was to be launched from the ship had a wing broken off when a hook to launch it was not caught properly, the plane was wrecked. When this

SHIP'S LOG

happened the ship was in Lisbon, Portugal. They were in the harbor when a liner of great importance was leaving the dock. The liner was near the Dutch warship when suddenly the wind arose and the liner banged into the warship, causing damage that sent the warship into dry dock for six weeks in Spain. All of these disasters were humiliating for the finest Dutch ship.

When he returned to see his parents, he was shocked.

Cornelus spent four years near the Shetland Islands and Norway on the submarines. Their periscope was shot off by a torpedo plus other top parts of the sub. This was friendly fire. It was a miracle they survived. When he returned to Holland after the war to see his parents, he was shocked. His mother was just skin stretched over her bones. She had sold most of their belongings to buy food. The food was potatoes and cabbage when it was available.

Friday - December 11th, 1992

We arrive in Houston and received a "Welcome Home."

I have an airline ticket from Houston to Minneapolis to Fargo on Northwest Airlines arranged by the Captain by telex from out at sea. This is a $360 ticket paid for by Ivaran. A van picked me up at the gang plank and took me to the airport. Customs came on board at 9:30 this morning but no problems arose. Immigration just looked at my passport and said, "Welcome Home." Immigration is very strict.

A $5,000 fine for a visa oversight.

My English friend did not have a visa for the U.S. When foreigners fly here they do not need one but when they arrive by ship it is required. Immigration put a man with him the whole day to be sure he boarded a British Airways plane to return to England. This causes a $5,000.00 fine for the ship that he did not have a U.S. visa.

On another ship some passengers got off to see a doctor. They did not have their shore passes and that ship

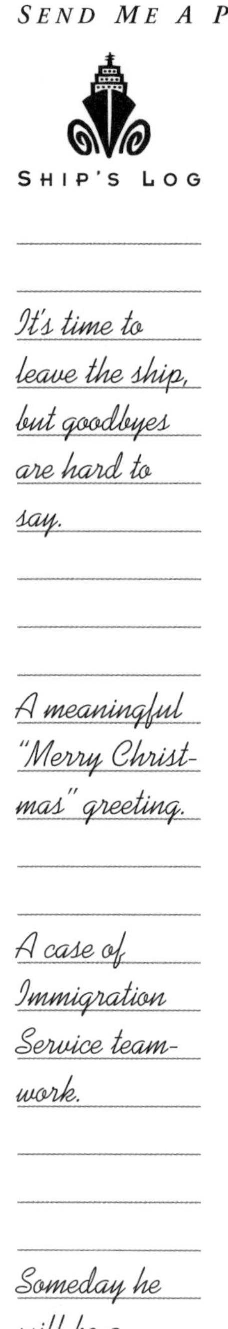

was fined $8,000.00. Our Captain had been told that the Englishman did not need a visa to come here. The Argentina office gave him this information. Wrong!

Before leaving the ship I got up early, dressed in my best red suit in honor of Christmas and said goodbye to almost everyone. Even went down to the crew mess hall to say goodbye to those who do the dirty work. An older Mexican got tears in his eyes when I said, "Adios, Amigo." Many times when I walked the lower deck we would chat. He in Spanish, me in English. I would give him a pack of cigarettes.

Another crew member wanted to say Merry Christmas to me in English but could not remember how to say it. As he held my hand one of his pals helped him say it. Joe, the radio man, took me through his office and gave me a long history of a plant he is nurturing. He says it blooms one day a year and fills the house with a sweet aroma.

There was a Rumanian stowaway who came off one of the ships. Immigration caught him and assigned two men on him until he could be sent back. One man watching him was tall and thin. The other was a large, muscular Mexican. Their theory was that if the stowaway tried to run away, the tall, skinny guy could catch him and the muscular guy could hold him down. I laughed about this but the ship was fined $8,000.00. Many foreigners are desperate to come here.

There is a young fellow on the ship, 19 years old. He is a beginning trainee to become an officer. He is given many dirty jobs. His name is Stephen Jensen and he comes from northern Norway. He wants to be a Captain someday. The old salts tease him and tell him to get a decent job. They say he can be a policeman. It is steady

I'm glad I took the trip.

work arresting the drunks in Norway. He pays no attention.

I'm glad I had the courage to take this trip. It was unusual to be the only American aboard. I knew images of Charles would flash before me often but feel it is part of the healing process.

Now it is almost Christmas. It is time to prepare for the holiday and pet the cat. My favorite Christmas story is Dickens' Christmas Carol. My favorite character is Tiny Tim. I shall close with his famous quote:

"God Bless Us Everyone."

CHAPTER IV

A Coastal Steamer Adventure In Norway

October 1993

—

November 1993

MS MIDNATSOL

Our sailing date on the coastal steamer Midnatsol was September 27, 1993 and lasted for 15 days. The ship was built in 1982 and rebuilt in 1988. It has space for 40 cars and 322 passengers. Named for the Midnight Sun, it is a beautiful, clean ship with a lovely observation deck. The steamer carries mail and freight. The cost for airline tickets, train tickets, hotels, and meals was approximately $3,420.

Ship's Log

Pay close attention and your luggage may end up where you go.

I was determined to go in spite of some afflictions.

New Jersey airports don't mind smokers.

Chapter IV

Norway - September 27th, 1993
The Midnightsol Coastal Steamer

Getting into a mode of traveling alone to places where you know no one, can be scary, but just do it. There are two rules that are helpful when traveling alone. Be early and know your itinerary well. Know airports, railroad stations, hotels and ships. If I had not caught an airport agent booking my luggage to Heathrow Airport, London, instead of Gatwick, there would have been much trauma for me. We travelers usually end up in the right place but often our luggage doesn't.

Marcia took me to the airport in Fargo. Northwest Airline checked my suitcase all the way to Oslo. That was most helpful. Going on this trip has been iffy due to three days ago something twitched in my head and for a time it affected my vision and balance. Seeing a doctor did not appeal to me. He may have discouraged me from leaving the country. Since plans had been in the works for five months and all the necessary tickets were paid for and in my possession, it was too late not to go. Only a broken leg would put a stop to it.

The flight to Minneapolis is smooth. All I am responsible for is a small carry-on bag and my purse. When we arrive there, I don't have to walk a mile to a gate - the same plane goes to Newark. You can even have a cigarette in the Newark airport. New Jersey has not condemned us for this habit.

"Norwegians have tough mothers."

There is a lot of time until my next flight so I sit by a young security guard, we smoke and visit. When people are told I am going to Norway, many claim to have Norwegian blood. Don't you believe it! They only wish they had Norwegian blood. The young security guard tells me that Norwegians are gentlemen because they have tough mothers. He said when his grandmother took her children to the beach, she had a rope and would lasso the children if they got too far away. It was a good story.

The plane's crew were all Norwegians.

There was a bus to take passengers to the overseas flight gates. The plane was a DC 9 and the Captain and flight attendants were all Norwegian. So were almost all of the passengers. Flight attendants were well-groomed. They were not young glamour women but were a bit older, attractive and competent. This was about a seven to eight hour flight. Cocktails were served and a fine dinner. I am sitting by a large screen that shows how many miles we have flown, how many more to go and other details. I'm in a non-smoking section and that is acceptable but I'm getting restless and I walk to the back and ask the stewardess if I can have a cigarette. She says, "Oh my, no, but you can sit and have one." There was no place to sit so I went back to my seat and watched the screen.

Going through customs was a breeze.

We arrive in Oslo. It is clean and modern. First, I check into the country, pick up my luggage and go through customs. Since I had nothing to declare it was a breeze.

A quick lesson on Norwegian money.

Next, it was necessary to find the money exchange and trade American dollars for kroner. The exchange is about seven kroner for one dollar. Next, I must find a bus to take me to a hotel where I have a reservation. Outside is an S.A.S. bus. This is Scandinavian Air Service. This is the hotel where I am to stay. The bus driver is a handsome, young fellow with a charming accent. He says he

It felt good to crawl under the covers.

My Norwegian connection in Oslo made for a pleasant time.

I am relieved to find the train.

I had a seat reservation but that didn't matter to that pushy group.

may not go to this hotel this trip. He gives me a lesson about the value of the krone. I prolong my questions just to hear him speak.

Another American from Connecticut also wants to go to the S.A.S hotel. The bus driver agrees to take us there. We had to negotiate and ended up paying about six dollars. That is about 42 kroner. Checking into the hotel was no problem and accommodations very fine. After flying all night, it felt good to crawl under the covers.

Oslo is a city of 450,000. Drive-by shootings are unknown and muggings are rare. I had a telephone number of a young working couple. I had not met this couple but there was a connection. They are friends of John and Kathy Needham who are friends of mine. They came to the hotel to get me and we went for dinner. Their two year old daughter, Gina, was with us. It was a pleasing evening. They shared a lot of their feelings and I fell for Gina, a blonde, blue-eyed child. They invited me to their home for butterscotch schnapps and coffee. Gina sat in my lap and we read some of her books. Some were in English. I could read a little of the animal Norwegian books and some about trains and trucks. She hugged me when we said good-bye. It was her bed time.

In the morning I had to rise early, check out of the hotel and leave for the railroad station. A taxi solved this trip. The reservation was for wagon 11 (cars in Norway are called wagons), track three and seat 52. It was another relief to find the train.

Alas! Someone is in my seat. A tour guide has put all her people in seats that have been reserved previously by others. I was burning inside but tried not to show it. The man in my seat was an overweight, ugly American. He brushed me off by telling me these seats had been

reserved some time ago. I kept my cool and remarked I would just stand there until it was resolved.

The tour guide of this group approached me with an "in your face" speaking Norwegian. I am able to understand a little Norwegian but she spoke fast and in a most firm manner. I did not back off and told her I did not understand what she was saying. She switched to English and I still did not back off. The final result was adding another wagon to the train to accommodate this group. It was just a private, catty feeling that I enjoyed thoroughly. I got the seat assigned to me.

The train was very comfortable. There is a lot of leg room, walk around space and the cart comes by with soft drinks and open-faced sandwiches. Coffee is available at all times without charge. The cost for an open-faced sandwich and a bottle of soda is $8.00. This is an eight hour trip ...destination Bergen. Most of my sandwich fell on the floor.

Traveling across Norway shows rugged terrain of mountains, glaciers, rivers and small farms of cattle and sheep. There are small grain fields in the valleys. It all looks so peaceful but maybe these farms have problems like the farms in the U.S.

We arrive in Bergen at 6:30 p.m. I must get a taxi to the ship. At the cab stand many people are waiting. There were so many, I did not know if I would ever get a cab but people were polite and they knew when it was my turn. Quite gracious, I must say.

The harbor is not far. We get there in 10 minutes. I walk up the gang way and get checked in by a young stewardess. She takes me to Cabin 322 which was assigned to me three months earlier. There is an American woman in there and she is all unpacked. The stew-

I hope that the ship doesn't leak like my glass does!

A bouquet of flowers tells me that all is going to be alright.

My new friend is interesting and certainly well-traveled.

ardess is embarrassed and goes to an office to check on it. I am getting bucky and am tired. The office says there is something wrong with my ticket and assign me to Cabin 411. I tell them if it does not have a window I won't accept it, but it does.

After a flight to Oslo and an eight-hour train ride to Bergen, I'm ready to pour myself a drink. The plastic glass leaks and it all runs down the sink. Drat! Drinks here are $8.00 each or 56 kroner. I try the other glass and it, too, leaks. What a conundrum! This is a neat, clean, small cabin but the glasses leak and there are no towels. It did not take long to go down to the desk and ask for a "glass" glass and towels. The door to the cabin stuck, too, and it took the strength of Atlas to open it. I'm in a livid mood by this time. Talking to myself helps some.

I go to the dining room for a light meal. There is much banter there and someone tells me a lovely bouquet has arrived for me. I don't get my hopes up that I have a secret admirer. No such luck! The bouquet was exquisite with orchids and was sent by my travel agency. The door to my cabin did open, glasses and towels were delivered, too.

In the dining area, my assigned table is with a woman from London and two couples from Western Australia. The London lady, Dorothy, and I took walking hikes into some of the cities. The coastal steamer docks at every town to leave or pick up mail and freight.

Dorothy was a nurse in World War II. She has traveled to places I haven't even heard of. Her husband owned a heavy machinery factory. He died long ago. She is from a long established Jewish family who came back to England at the time Oliver Cromwell was allowing Jews into the country.

One of her sons is an Oxford graduate. He recently married a gentile woman. Dorothy would prefer the blood lines to be kept pure but that is not to be. She gave them an elaborate reception at a fine hotel.

She and I eat together and sometimes share wine with dinner. She told me a story of her nursing days. She was walking ashore in Italy and met two American Naval Officers. They invited her as a guest to an aircraft carrier. She was the only woman on the carrier. The dinner was a huge steak. She was awed by this and said, "We Britons had never seen anything like it."

Dorothy thinks I am running away from life with my travels. There has been plenty to run away from at times. Perhaps she is right.

She and I hiked into Alesund to see the shops and get our feet on the ground. Beautiful objects of crystal, silver, china and wool tempted us but we were strong and did not buy.

At Trondheim we took a bus into the city to a music museum. There were many ancient instruments and up to the 20th century. A young music student gave the lecture. In the Beethoven room she played "Fur Elise". There was a Chopin room and there we heard some of his well-known melodies. In the Edvard Grieg room she played a lullaby. In the Mozart room we were treated to a sonata. This was all much to our liking.

Don't know how the Europeans wash their ears. There are no wash cloths. The plumbing baffles me. Some knobs and buttons you push, some you pull, some you twist and some you do all of the above. For God's sake, don't flush the toilet while you are sitting on it. It can suck out your innards. What an ugly thought. It has happened, I suspect. It could be a slow death.

Fish is plentiful, and we are plenty full of fish.

There has been no profound conversation. I try to get the stewardess to chat with me but her duties are more pressing. One of them thinks I am related to Errol Flynn and treats me like royalty. I tell her it is not so but she prefers to believe it.

You will laugh when yesterday there was fish soup for dinner, fish for the main course and fish for lunch. Today we got down to meatballs. Serious stuff.

We crossed the Arctic Circle this morning at 8:54 o'clock. This steamer provides a smooth ride. We have a deck with a panoramic view giving us a full look at the fjords and mountains. We come within a few feet of these cliffs.

October 1st, 1993 - Tromso, Norway

The Capital of the North.

This is a city of 50,000 and is considered the Capital of the North. We went on a tour here to a museum that had much art beadwork and showed a lot of the culture of the Sami people. They are the northern reindeer people. The tour took us to a Lutheran Cathedral with huge windows of tinted glass. It was shaped like a triangle. I saw only a smattering of hymn books.

These friends from "down under" are free spirits and so are their drinks.

The Australians are in the lounge mixing their own drinks. This is frowned upon but these people are free spirits and know how to have fun. They have traveled the world. One family has a travel agency and the other is a CPA and has accounts in several countries. They think I am hard of hearing because I ask them to repeat what they say. I am not hard of hearing but their accents are not familiar to me and take a moment to decipher.

Some of us took a bus to the North Cape. It is the farthest north place in Europe with roads to arrive by car. I expected a small trading post but what a surprise. There was a huge building with shops, a fine restaurant and a

SHIP'S LOG

The midnight sun makes for some long days.

A party is missed just by accent-idently.

Heaven help me and my strange eating habits.

theater in the round. In the theater we saw a film of northern culture including birds, flowers, weather, ships and seasons. We had several hours here. It was foggy and we couldn't see far returning to the Midnightsol. It was scary in the fog traveling the mountain roads. This is the place of the midnight sun. At North Cape, the sun shines for 10 weeks without setting.

A couple from Florida is leaving the ship at Kirkenes. This is the farthest north place we sail. From there, they were to fly to Oslo and thence to Florida. Due to fog, the plane did not take off. It was seven hours until the next flight. Their other choice was to rent a car and drive 300 kilometers to the next airport. We did not find out what they chose to do.

Before they left the ship some of us were to gather to chat, say good-bye and wish them a safe trip. I looked for them in two of the lounges but did not see them and went back to my cabin. Dorothy Lane says I am a lemon for not coming to the gathering. It was held on the observation deck. With the English accent and the Australian accents there was a communication difficulty.

We are now sailing south again. The food is every kind you can name. Dorothy is shocked I eat a boiled egg and toast and jam in the morning. She says it does not go together. Also, I drink a glass of milk for lunch. She says milk is for calves, not good for us. You do not mix fish and meat either. Heaven help me, I have even used the wrong spoon for soup and dessert and tipped my soup bowl the wrong way. Will I never learn?

The lock on my door sticks and won't open. The coded card just does not work. Four times I have had to ask a crew member for help. Today it would not open for them either. The Chief Engineer had to put on a new lock. It took an hour.

SHIP'S LOG

"The whole world cried."

A rear-view mirror may offer a clue.

The Ginger Tree is outstanding!

Judge not, lest ye be also judged.

Coffee at the cafeteria costs about $1.60 American. The young bartender's name is Roy. He is reading a book about the coastal steamers and how one sunk in 1962. All the lives were lost. It was the same week Kruschev was sending ships to Cuba loaded with missiles. JFK challenged Kruschev and the Russian ships were turned back. I tell Roy I wept when JFK was shot. He says his mother wept bitter tears and added, "The whole world cried."

There is an American tour group on board. They are an elderly group and not particularly friendly or outgoing. Their dress is most unattractive. This is not the place to be a fashion model, but tight polyester pants on fat women? Ugh! The rear view is appalling.

Yesterday we had potato dumplings. I ate two of them. Dorothy thinks I am mad. She calls pudding nursery food. We do get along well and I like her.

Among the books I have read are Studs Lonnigan, about an Irish family in Chicago during the depression and The Ginger Tree by Oswald Wynd. This book is outstanding and I am sorry to say good-bye to the characters.

Just bought a bus ticket to go from the ship to my hotel in Bergen. This is the S.A.S. Royal Hotel. The bus ticket cost was $3.60.

In London, Dorothy says she never goes near the Irish pubs. The pubs attract the working class and they get drunk and rowdy. Should we have the right to judge these people?

In Bergen where passengers disembarked there were buses to take us to hotels. My hotel was the S.A.S. and friend Dorothy was staying at the Orion Hotel. She and I walked and window shopped. For the evening meal at the hotel, a hamburger, fries and a glass of wine cost $14.00. My flight to Oslo was scheduled at 8:30 a.m.

They were having one helluva good time.

This was canceled due to mechanical failure and the delay was one hour.

Oslo airport was confusing to me this time and as I stumbled through security my purse was forgotten on the tray. Discovering this scared the hell out of me and I had to scramble to go way back to security and retrieve it. The plane left on time and I was most relieved to be on it. This was a seven hour flight. The plane was full of Norwegians and many of them were going on holiday. They were having one helluva good time.

Arriving in Newark was a mad house. Got through immigration and waiting for luggage was slow and tiresome. I could not get my bag checked through to Fargo unless an S.A.S. agent tagged it. I scurried around to find an S.A.S. agent and finally did. The fellows checking luggage assured me my bag would go to Fargo and nowhere else.

The stop at Newark has its ups and downs for me.

This is a huge building and I ask questions. To find the Northwest section one employee told me to go up two flights and to the left. The only thing up there was an ice cream and popcorn stand. I was told to go down one flight and to the right. After three tries I finally found it. In the line a Chinese couple stepped directly in front of me. My blood pressure zoomed and I'm livid but kept my cool.

Crossing the Arctic Circle was a chilling experience!

Forgot to write earlier of the big "Cross the Arctic Circle" party. There was a comic ceremony by King Neptune. We had to kneel and many screams were heard as a dipper of ice cubes was put down our shirts. We were given a small glass of liquor and a certificate confirming the cross of the Arctic Circle.

It is still a thrill to come home.

Arriving in Fargo was wonderful. In Minneapolis there were fifty gates to walk. This called for an electric car. As much violence as there is in the U.S.A., it is still a thrill to come home. Norwegians are lucky to live in a safe environment but home is still home.

CHAPTER V

The MV San Antonio's Fourth Voyage

October 1994

—

December 1994

MV SAN ANTONIO

This new ship was built in Germany for Ivaran Lines and carries 1500 containers and 12 passengers. It has luxury accomodations and the cost of a round trip in 1995 was $6,690. Previous passengers receive a generous discount. The MV San Antonio sails from the United States to Buenos Aires, "The Paris of Latin America"

SHIP'S LOG

"...always one foot of water under the keel."

Clean to perfection and elegant.

A nice welcome to a smooth sail.

Chapter V

October 1st, 1994 - MS San Antonio

"On the occasion of her maiden voyage to Buenos Aires - with best wishes for good luck, calm seas and always one foot of water under the keel."

– *Agencia Maritima Robinson S.A.*
Buenos Aires, April 26, 1994

The above plaque is found in the lounge of the MV San Antonio, a Norwegian container ship that sails from Port Elizabeth, New Jersey, to Buenos Aires, Argentina. Now the San Antonio is on her fourth voyage. She carried 12 passengers, about 25 officers and crew and almost 1500 containers of freight. As one of the passengers, I find this ship to be clean to perfection and elegant.

The passengers are looked after by the Chief Steward. He does his best to keep us all comfortable and happy. My cabin is about ten feet wide and twenty feet long. It is decorated in a dark red carpet and green and gold sofa and drapes. There is a television, VCR, refrigerator, radio, hair dryer, ample storage, telephone, and air conditioning.

Upon arrival I found fresh flowers, champagne and a white terry cloth bathrobe with the San Antonio logo. So far, sailing has been smooth, making it hard to remember I am on a ship. We left Port Elizabeth in the night and the first stop was Baltimore. There was enough time for a tour of the city and lunch. Four of us took the tour. The

SHIP'S LOG

This sparked our patriotism.

Another history lesson in Norfolk.

A quest for mint juleps.

driver and tour guide was a congenial fellow but did not know much about the city. We went to Fort McHenry and tramped through the Visitors Center and the Fort.

We watched a film of the 1812-1814 battles with the British Fleet and the origin of our National Anthem. This was quite moving and sparked our patriotism. A passenger from Norfolk knew much more of the city than the tour guide and filled us in on many interesting details. It was fun and lunch put us all in a happy mood. Crab cakes are the food to order but in my mind they would be like a meatball with crab instead of beef. That didn't sound so great to me.

In our group was an elderly woman from Pasadena and a teacher from Colorado. The gentleman from Norfolk is a retired teacher also and is an expert on east coast history. He has a bit of that charming southern accent. From now on, I shall call him Jack.

When we docked at Norfolk he gave a history lesson of the city, the harbor and most of the ships in it. There were three aircraft carriers, including the "Eisenhower" and the "Enterprise." He is having his election ballot mailed to Buenos Aires. The senate race in Virginia is expensive, close and one of the candidates is Oliver North. He thinks it is a done deal that North will win.

I have no calendar and have no idea what the date is. On board is a dietician from Cleveland. She is overwhelmed by all of this. There is a Jewish couple. Her voice is so sugary sweet, I cringe when she speaks. These are all only first impressions.

We are approaching Savannah and some of us plan to go ashore for dinner tonight. Wilma, from Pasadena; Wanda, from Colorado; and I went into the city to find a place that served mint juleps. We were not successful

People are out having fun!

I take a razzing about the climate of my state.

They made the Captain angry.

The handsome first mate says he will not let me drown.

but settled for bowls of lemon garlic shrimp. The river walk was teeming with people as Oktoberfest was being celebrated. I have never seen this many black people in my life. They are everywhere. In Fargo, ND, where I live we have very few and I don't know a single one. This city was busy. There were dinner boats, food stands, beer stands solid along the river. People are out having fun.

Our next stop is Miami. The harbor is large and spectacular. Some went into the city to a shopping mall but for me, it was too hot! I am taking a razzing about the climate of my state but yet they say we should have a reunion there. Surely they jest. Jack says he is waiting for me to say, "Come, ya all!" When I walked into happy hour last night, someone yelled, "Fix her a double martini. Anyone from North Dakota has to drink martinis to keep warm." Some of these people had never met anyone from North Dakota. They cannot believe we plug in our cars in the winter so they will start on a cold day. Naive, eh?

October 4th, 1994

We are sailing between Cuba and Haiti. I'm surprised the U.S. Coast Guard has not harassed us about cargo, destination, business and a host of information. They did this on an earlier trip and the Captain was angry.

We have just had a fire drill. I was to go to the lifeboat on the port side. We scrambled into our life jackets and entered a state-of-the-art life boat, all self-contained. It had rations, water, seat belts, radar, flares, material for smoke signals and more. The first mate is from Uruguay. Handsome. If I ever have to drown, I wouldn't mind drowning with him. He says, "Stick with me, you won't drown." We were taught how to jump into the water if the need should arise. Stay calm. First rule. Jack threatened to take my picture with my life jacket on. He thinks

SHIP'S LOG

The largest shipping company is from Denmark.

The Captain's dinner was a special delight.

My face was red, but not from being embarrassed.

I have never seen water before. His life boat was on the starboard side so the teasing subsided.

There is great competition here in the Atlantic for freight. The largest shipping company is from Denmark named Mersk. Their ships and containers are in all the ports. They have bought space at the docks. The other companies must pay large fees each time their ships dock. Ivaran has a lot of trade but not enough. They have sold off some of their ships. This is a new ship built in Germany and carries 1500 containers. We do not have a full load now but did have until we reached Miami. We carry 450 metric tons of fuel and use about 48 tons per day. We clip along at 20 knots. While checking with the Chief Engineer, we actually carry 1800 metric tons of fuel and refueling is done in New York.

The Captain's dinner is a special event and we dressed a little better; however, it was still casual. Cocktails were served from 5 to 6 o'clock and then dinner. Food included shrimp, lobster, lutefisk, prime rib, many salads and potatoes. The dessert was called Don Pedro consisting of ice cream and liquor. After the meal everyone socialized until midnight and there was coffee and brandy. The next party will be crossing the Equator.

We docked at Puerto Cabello, Venezuela, October 6th in the morning. There were many ships from different countries. Harbors filled with ships fascinate me. It was quite a sight and very hot by my standards. Wilma asked me to sit in the shade on the deck and share a bottle of champagne. This soft life could easily become a habit. As Wilma removed the cork, it went flying into the water. Naturally, since we had no cork we had to polish it off. I did not sit in the sun but my face turned bright red. The sun's rays bounce off the water. With my red face and frizzed-up hairdo, I was a mess. Next evening we docked

SHIP'S LOG

I can hold my own at card games.

Dangerous cargo and pirates.

Antonio is a master at the grill.

We make fun of ourselves and everyone else.

at La Guaira, Venezuela. There were city lights all in the hills and mountains. Such beauty. Being on deck was a must at this time. Our next stop is Rio de Janeiro, Brazil.

Some of us have played simple card games in the evening. One game is called Red Dog and another is Uno. This is accompanied by much laughter. Jack teases me at every opportunity but so far, I can hold my own.

Today we had a tour of part of the ship. The Captain explained some points of cargo, how the containers are placed and why. Dangerous cargo loading is all regulated and labeled. Also, he told us how pirates get aboard and how they hide in the inlets. The pirates demand access to the safe. Ships carry much cash but some is hidden in other places because of theft. It costs as much as $10,000 to dock at these ports. This included the pay of the stevedores.

We had the "Cross the Equator" party on the deck. It was very windy but everyone made the best of it. The cook's name is Antonio and he is a master at it. He is from Spain. He had two large grills and on them were chicken, sausage, beef ribs, barbecue pork ribs, tenderloin, sweet bread and something he called trip. Trip didn't look good and I didn't have it. There were rolls and salads and provalone cheese in foil which was heated and soft. Svend tells me if I come on the Christmas run next year I can help him with the Christmas baking.

Jack and I laugh at the same things and make fun of ourselves and everyone else. This is not malicious but funny to us. I continue to enjoy Wilma. The deck party was over about 10:30 but I'm sure the crew carried on until all hours. They never seem to wear out. One female passenger is flaky but most of the time treats me well. Another is quite taken with clothes and jewels and changes several times a day.

SHIP'S LOG

Some of the crew of previous trips have gone separate ways.

This ship is a thirsty one.

I usually miss seeing the whales or porpoises.

Some information comes to me about people of past trips. Ron Andreason has lost his chief steward job due to selling off of some ships.

10 o'clock weather bulletin:

Air temp	83 F
Sea temp	83 F.
Overcast	
Strong breeze	22 knots

Svend has a daughter, eleven months old. He is very proud of this. Dimitri is on another ship somewhere. Fabiana is a secretary in a mental hospital. She has a Norwegian boyfriend and wants to live in Norway. She got into the world of drugs. It is not known what became of Laura. She wanted to become an interpreter.

I bothered Ernst for some ship information and he converted metric tons to gallons for me. The fuel consumption of this ship is 13,473 of fuel oil each 24 hours. Fuel oil consumption round trip Newark-Buenos Aires-Newark is 375,000 gallons. Cylinder oil consumption round trip is 3,700 gallons. Fresh water consumption round trip is 205,000 gallons. Ernst says if I want to know how many chickens we eat round trip I must check with Svend. He, too, teases me but we laugh a lot.

There is quite a lot of wind on the decks. The weather bulletin has been air temp 86 F. Sea temp 83,. Southeast breeze October 12th, 19.8 knots. Next day it was 82 air temp, 81 sea temp and a strong wind of 25 knots from the southeast. Sometimes over the loud speaker the Captain will announce whales or porpoises to port or starboard. By the time I get out there they could be in Africa. Usually, I miss seeing them.

A flaky lady is giving me barbs quite often about unimportant things. Hopefully, I can handle it with

grace. Jack does not swear that I know about but he told me to tell her it is none of her goddamned business.

The last three evenings I have been watching movies. There is a wide selection from which to choose. The ones I saw are "The Firm," "Made in America," and Charles Dickens' "Christmas Carol."

I'm guessing the date is October 14th. We may go into Rio this afternoon. Some women want to go to the jewelry store again. Their bank accounts must be unlimited. How lucky I am to live in North Dakota, even if we are the blizzard capital of North America. These South American cities are over-crowded. In Rio, there are people jammed together wherever we look.

There is an interesting Catholic Cathedral with huge, stained-glass windows from base to peak and it is high. It must seat thousands. The tour took us to Sugar Loaf Mountain. We go to the top on a cable car. There are shops at the top selling over-priced tee shirts and trinkets for tourists.

Sitting on the deck as we leave the port of Rio is a thrilling experience! There are mountains, ships, coastlines, bridges, water and a city teeming with activity. This is evening and the lights are endless. Jack is wearing a ridiculous hat to keep the moon out of his eyes. When I twitted him about it, he took it off, turned it inside out and put it back on again. We say goodbye to Rio.

Next stop - Santos, Brazil. Here I receive some personal mail and a Newsweek magazine. It is a comfort to find out all is well at home.

This ship was anchored in the harbor two days before the Port Authority would allow us to dock. Only one couple went into the city to walk and have lunch.

No Excuses! Svend told me I was going

I had coffee with the Captain.

Sometimes I must back away from people and hide awhile in my cabin. Others believe I'm anti-social or pouting about something but this is not the reason. I need time to gather my wits and stay silent.

October 18th

We are drawing near Buenos Aires and should dock there October 19th around 7:00 a.m. There is a city tour at 9:00 a.m. I tell Svend I don't wish to go and he sticks his finger in my face and tells me I am going. No excuses! Gregory, the radio man, helped me and we tried to call the Marchi family in southern Brazil but we could not reach them. I had coffee with the Captain in his office and he tells me how fond he is of Norwegian food like rømmegrøt, krumkake and lefse. He says I should be living in Norway if I can make that kind of food. Also, could I send him some krumkake which in English means crumb cake. One stewardess, a Brazilian named Isolda, is leaving the ship in B.A. to have two months off.

Isolda: a stewardess from Brazil.

SHIP'S LOG

I can't figure out what to complain about.

She works in the dining room and the laundry but has many other duties, too, and is often exhausted. She works too hard for what she is paid and always has enough strength to kiss a cheek or tweak an ear. She is precious. The other stewardess is from B.A. and has six sisters. She does a lot of cabin work. Three of her sisters are named Maria, for a constellation, I believe. Svend can't figure out why I never complain about anything and I can't figure out what to complain about.

October 19th, 1994 - Buenos Aires Harbor

These handsome children touched me deeply.

We were taken to the Catholic City Cathedral. It is a unique, majestic place with much sculpture, stone work, intricate wood carving and stained glass. There were about a dozen children present wearing short white gowns. They, too, were on a tour from a Catholic school and wear the white to eliminate economic and social status. They clustered around me and had so many questions. My Spanish is good for only a few phrases but one of the older girls spoke some English. They were interested in how we came, what states we were from and would have visited all day if we had more time. These were handsome, well-behaved children. They wanted to hold hands and rub cheeks. Their skin and eyes are mostly darker than ours and oh, so pretty. Many of the earlier settlers came here from Spain, but other European countries, too. This was an experience that touched me deeply.

The Paris of Latin America.

Buenos Aires is known as The Paris of Latin America. The traffic in this city is the worst I have ever seen. We came close to having two crashes. One of the cars was that of the American ambassador. There is a law that the last two digits of an auto license plate determines what day a driver is allowed to enter the city. Not all who wish can drive into the city whenever they wish. Fines are imposed for ignoring the ordinance.

SHIP'S LOG

47 ships were waiting to dock.

Pirates invade our ship at night!

The Captain is forced to hand over much cash.

Monday - October 24th

We arrived in the harbor of Santos headed north. We will be anchored in the harbor a minimum of two days. We see 47 ships from all over the world waiting to dock. We must wait our turn and won't be registered until the anchor goes down. It is mild and some of us enjoyed the deck this night.

While eating dinner I get a telephone call. I prayed it didn't come from the U.S.A. It was Angela Marchi calling from southern Brazil. I had to rush to the radio room to take this call. The other passengers raise their eyebrows when I get this call. Angela tells me they cannot come to Santos at this time.

This night was a sleepless one for me. After 3:00 a.m. I did begin to nod off. There are three guards on this ship and it is well lit at night. However, this night, October 25th, at 1:30 a.m. eight pirates invaded the ship. They came in the dark of night in a small boat. They throw a hook over the stern and can climb up in eight seconds. They overpowered a guard before he could warn anyone, held a knife to his head and forced him to take them to the Captain.

The Captain, too, is threatened and they demand he open the safe. I was awake at this time and heard doors open and close and once even suspected someone tried my door. There are many noises on this ship and I can't be sure of anything. The Captain was forced to take them to the vault. Ships carry much cash but luckily, it was not all in the vault. A large amount of cash was taken. It is not known how much.

Also, the pirates took watches from the officers. No one was hurt. It is not known if the guard was a part of the conspiracy. It is of little use to report it to the police

SHIP'S LOG

Our ship chooses the safety of the open sea.

Few freighters carry passengers... that probably saved our jewelry and cash!

We set up shop in my cabin.

or Port Authority. They shrug their shoulders and say, "So what? People get robbed every day." Even when customs and immigration come aboard, there are bribes with whiskey and cigarettes. If the Captain does not give gifts, small infractions are threatened with fines to follow. It can be as insignificant as a typo error on a report.

I had a premonition that pirates would come aboard but did not dare say anything for fear of being laughed at and ridiculed. After it was all over, I told the Captain of my premonition and he replied, "Shit! Then it is your fault." After the pirates left, the Captain pulls up anchor, the engines start and we head for open sea. It is felt there is more safety there. Is it closing the barn door after the horse got out? The Captain says they can hit two nights in a row.

October 27th

We come to the dock. All day, unloading and loading is going on. We leave again tonight for Rio. That is another harbor full of danger. Pirates lurk in the inlets. The pirates, perhaps, did not know there were passengers aboard. Few freighters carry them. They could have demanded any jewelry and cash. If they had harassed passengers a foreign government could become involved, but this is only speculation.

Jack, from Norfolk, has been fussing about his hair getting too long and fuzzy around the neck and ears. After listening to this for several days, I tell him to get some scissors and I would get the job done. He did and I did. We set up shop in my cabin. We left the door open so anyone could observe and the remarks were hilarious. Some scurried for their cameras.

I announced that I had no training in hair cutting and had not done it for 30 years when I turned a bowl

SHIP'S LOG

There was much teasing, but business was booming.

The oldest city in South America greets us with garbage.

Our ankles will soon be black and blue.

over my sons' heads and just cut off what hung down. Some thought I was crazy to do it and Jack was crazy to allow it. There has been much teasing but it went remarkably well. Even trimmed his eyebrows. One fellow asked if I would trim the hair on his legs. The Chief Engineer requested a haircut but he had these unmanageable curls sticking out in every direction and I was reluctant to tackle the job. Svend told me to cut hair in the bathroom but nix on that. The bathroom is too small. Jack says when he gets home he will tell his barber a cattle-grain rancher from North Dakota cut his hair. He will make a good story of it.

Today is November 2nd, 1994

We left Fortaleza, Brazil on a straight run to New York. We were in Salvador a few days ago and some of us took a tour of the city. This is the oldest city in South America. There is the rich part and the poor part. Some young men threw garbage at our van.

This is perfect weather for sitting on the deck evenings. Near the equator there is much humidity.

When I see Jack getting annoyed at the dinner table I give him a kick under the table. He does the same to me. Our ankles will soon be black and blue. At the other table one passenger has a hang up on her fur coats and jewels. Nancy says if this goes on much longer, she will stand, throw her hands up and yell, "Bullshit!" I wait to see that. Nancy and Jimmy are fun people. They tell me they would like to retire in North Dakota. I tell them they must be affected by the humidity.

In Forteleza we went to a beach. There are palm trees and thatched huts. Food and drinks are served and there is much for sale. There was lace, linen, shoes, handbags, jewelry and almost anything handmade or otherwise. We

We are very near the Equator.

Melussi gave me a big hug.

These ships carry a wide variety of freight.

I become an adopted Confederate... perhaps I'll sing "Dixie."

sat at tables by the beach and had Coca-Cola. Ernst had Brahma beer and says it is quite good. Svend seated us to his liking. He put me so I could look at Jack. He put Jack so he could see the scantily-clad young women. There was a good supply.

We are very near the Equator. Some of the women stayed a longer time to shop. We are soon into another Equator barbecue.

Time to do laundry again and I can't find the blue fabric softener. Patricia, a stewardess, says to ask Antonio, the cook. "He will help you." Antonio tells Melussi, the mess boy, to find it for me. Melussi cannot speak English so he waves his arms and says, "2-2-2-2." He is about 25 years old and looks younger. First, he gives me a big hug and then he finds the softener. He is dear.

There may be a curiosity as to what freight is being sent south and north in these 1,500 containers. Some on the list are auto parts, lube oil, frozen fish, ceramic tiles, leather, decor paper, resin, shoes, candy, machinery, coffee green, orange oil, copper, plastic laminates, wheels, magnets, electric motors, tire valves, fiberglass, cotton clothes, aluminum foil, sprayers, furniture, dog articles, tires, tea, flour, cashew nuts, coffee, diesel engines, truck parts, cotton yarn, lamps, tapes, and much more. A list was received - compliments of the Chief Mate.

Again, we did the "Cross the Equator" party. Nice night - no wind. Nancy has that southern accent and tells me, "You are not a Yankee or a Confederate woman. Don't ever lose your Dakota thinking and heritage. You are more like a Confederate so we are adopting you." They think North Dakota is heaven with a low, white population and free of traffic jams. My nickname now is Dakota and Nancy is going to name her dog after me. It's

The ship's bridge is a maze of high technology.

We're alerted to a possible hurricane.

a compliment? I have told them plenty about our flat, productive state.

Today was my first trip up to the bridge. What a place! Windows all around and much computer and radar equipment. It would take months of instructions to understand it all. We are headed on a straight course to New York. The young officer on duty is from Argentina and we call him Pin. How he came to be called that is a mystery when his name is Marcello. He explained some of the rudiments of navigation.

There is a tropical storm north of us that has been upgraded to a hurricane. The wind is 75 to 85 knots. It is not directly in our path but moving parallel to us in a northwesterly direction. Weather reports come every hour. There are alarm buttons that flash if anything anywhere on the ship shows a sign of trouble. There is a small stove, sink, couch and other comforts in a spacious set-

On the Bridge of MV San Antonio, with First Officer Marcello.

We go smack dab through the Bermuda Triangle!

The cargo's value was greater than the ship's.

What an impression I must have made.

Svend gave me a meaningful Christmas present.

ting. Visibility is possible for long distances. Pin tells us the Captain will change course if the storm threatens our path.

In the evening the Captain did change course, taking a more westerly route. We were originally on course for 60 to 80 nautical miles west of Bermuda but then it changed. We go smack-dab through the Bermuda Triangle. The officers make fun of the strange stories about that area.

After dinner there is some card playing but I'm enjoying the deck. Becoming restless, I head for the bridge again and on duty now is a young officer called Co-Co. He is also from Argentina. I'm interested in the progress of the storm. We were warned there would be some rolling and pitching. I had a premonition of a storm also but that we were not in danger. I said nothing for the same reason; people think you are crazy or unhitched. The cargo carried has a higher value than the value of the whole ship which is about 13 million dollars. The cargo is measured in tons.

Last evening was the Captain's farewell dinner. There was shrimp cocktail, lobster, steak, French onion soup and baked Alaska. After dinner Ernst, Svend, Jack and I sat in the lounge socializing. One passenger appeared in a gold lamé suit. This impressed me as my wardrobe was a black skirt for dress up and sloppy shorts and pants for every day. What an impression I must have made.

Svend has packed a box for me to take home and strict instructions not to open until Christmas Eve. Much later I can reveal that box contained a small Norwegian flag, a coffee pot, teapot, 2 cups and saucers of the ship's china. I was delighted.

SHIP'S LOG

Becoming a ship's officer is not easy or quick.

My ability must be apparent as I take over the steering of the ship!

Jack says my goal was to drive him crazy.

"Welcome Home."

November 7, 1994

This day the main thought is how to pack in the most painless, efficient way. Jack goes with me to the bridge again. Pin is on duty. He is 29 years old and qualified to be a Captain. To become an officer, first they must attend school, then serve a time at sea, attend more school and again serve at sea. Each advancement requires more school and more experience at sea. The Captain took training for four years at a special school in Norway. About 30 graduate at the highest rank each year. It is not easy to find jobs on a ship, even after graduating.

We are in a weather front of rain and the water is choppy. The Captain insists I sit in the big chair and change the course of the ship. It only requires turning a knob not much larger than a silver dollar. Turn counter-clockwise to turn right and clockwise to turn left. It is easier than driving a pickup truck. There is not a feeling of turning such a huge vehicle except the wake shows the change. We had coffee at the bridge and watched the rain. The view is spectacular.

Packing is not fun but the thought of returning home is wonderful. Jack says I only came on the ship to drive him crazy and I have done a good job of it! I am completely mystified as to how I accomplished this and had I known, perhaps would have pursued it even more vigorously.

The Newark airport has three terminals and I don't know even which one I leave out of. We got to New York at 1:00 a.m. I am wide awake, shower and dress because customs and immigration come aboard at 3:00 a.m. Each of us must meet with them. Our passports are returned at this time and our luggage was not inspected. The passport was stamped and the agent said, "Welcome Home."

Airports make me nervous.

Memories that I cherish.

It's hard to stay in touch with everyone.

He made it even by polishing my shoes..

I was on a high and couldn't think of sleep but the Captain said, "Go to Bed! Your limo is not coming until 11:00 a.m."

It was not a happy morning for me. The thought of going home was happy but touching three airports to get there made me apprehensive and jumpy. It was not easy to say goodbye to everyone. We had become quite close. Of course, it was Jack who cheered me some. He is a gentleman and said he would escort me to the proper terminal. Almost, but not quite, kept my composure.

There are some things I shall never forget. One was the look on Nancy's face when I said I had a high regard for General Robert E. Lee. Also, that most of the north felt this way. She sees many Yankee women as obnoxious and has no warm feelings for them. One thing that galls her was the making of a graveyard of Lee's estate. I have seen this and agree with her - how awful it is. She is planning to send me a confederate flag even if it is politically incorrect. (She did.)

Another memory is how close the stars appear to be while sitting on the deck at night. Just like you could reach out and grab one. We talk about staying in touch and our intentions are honorable but eventually we disengage ourselves and no longer communicate.

Jack and I were invited to Svend's cabin to see videos of his home in Norway and his baby daughter. It is an honor to be invited to an officer's cabin. The most hilarious event was cutting Jack's hair. Everyone enjoyed it and made fun. He reciprocated by polishing my shoes. It was an even trade.

One of the best things about a trip like this is the relaxation. Sleep when you want, eat when you are hungry, read all day if it pleases you or swim, walk the deck,

SHIP'S LOG

Midwesterners should take these trips.

No luck at the slots.

New York is quite a sight.

I enjoyed my brief visit to New Jersey.

socialize or write, as I have chosen to do. Ivaran has been carrying passengers since 1925. Midwesterners do not take these trips. They should. If you want a party boat, take a trip on the Americana. I have already described a trip on the San Antonio. Getting to know the officers, crew and passengers is the joyful part. I have invitations to come to several countries but right now my own bed and bath sound delicious.

Before this trip took place I flew to Newark and was met by Elizabeth Halverson from Shrewsbury, New Jersey. She and I are friends and her husband Jared was a cousin of my first husband. We had fun.

We went to the ocean and watched the breakers and had dinner at a waterfront cafe. We took the bus to Atlantic City and had lunch at an old famous hotel and tried our luck at the slots. No luck.

We took a commuter boat to New York and up the East River. We sailed by Ellis Island, the Statue of Liberty and under the famous bridges. The World Trade Center and all of the business sections were brightly lit. The bridges are well known and include the Verazanno, the Brooklyn, the Manhattan and the Williamsburg. It was quite a sight in a small boat.

New Jersey is the Garden State and I can see why. There are many horse farms and huge vegetable markets. We also went to Jared's grave and set a blooming plant. There were markers in this graveyard from the 1700s. Elizabeth and her son-in-law, Eric, drove me to the harbor to board the San Antonio. We had dinner aboard ship and it was neat to get a ride to the gang plank. It was a real joy to go aboard and see Svend, Ernst, Miquel and Antonio. There are more people I know and will meet later.

SHIP'S LOG

There is a verse that fits the goodbyes and farewells:

Rain on the windows
Creaking doors
And winds that besom the green.
And I am here
And you are there
And a hundred miles between.
– Thomas Hardy

CHAPTER VI

An Encore For The MV San Antonio

November 1995

—

January 1996

SHIP'S LOG

It was like coming home.

Many changes, changed my agenda.

Jack and I had a lot to talk about.

Chapter VI

November 27th, 1995 - Miami Harbor

The MV San Antonio docked in Norfolk, Virginia, November 24th, 1995. This was one day after Thanksgiving. I boarded at 2:00 p.m. I knew Svend, Harry, Eduardo, another Eduardo, Pin, Malussie, Isolda. Maria, one passenger and maybe more. Oh, yes, the cook, Antonio. They were all generous with their hugs and kisses. It was like coming home. When this trip ends, I will have spent six and one-half months at sea totally for all trips. November 19th I arrived in Norfolk by air and was met by a dear friend, Jack Langley. This was an early date to arrive but there are two reasons why.

First, I had planned to board in Newark and have a fun visit with my friend Elizabeth Halverson. She died suddenly, shortly before we were to get together. Second, I had changed my airline tickets twice due to the changing of docking dates.

Jack has not changed and still loves to tease. He told his friends I had 12 suitcases when I only had two. After checking into the Old Dominion Inn he took me to his home where he had prepared supper. He has cooked vegetable beef soup and baked brownies. There were also hot rolls and wine, all served most graciously. His sister Muriel ate with us and what a fine time it was. We had a lot to talk about.

The next morning he came to get me and cooked breakfast. I had a choice of at least five kinds of fruit. I

SHIP'S LOG

I could have spent days at The Mariner's Museum.

say, "Forget the prune." After, we went for a drive that took us through the Monitor Merrimac tunnel under the James River. This is a great engineering feat of modern times. It is dug 95 feet under the river that leads to Chesapeake Bay. Ocean-going vessels can sail over it.

The Mariner's Museum was our destination. This is an interesting museum with displays that would take days to absorb. We went by the Navy Yards where many ships were visible. Since Norfolk is the home of the Atlantic Fleet, it can be expected to see different and many ships. There were frigates, tenders and aircraft carriers. The carriers cost about three billion each to construct. Each one carries 6,500 personnel and 90 aircraft. They are nuclear powered and must be refueled about every fifteen years. This costs millions.

In the evening we enjoyed dinner at a seafood restaurant by the water. In the morning he came to get me

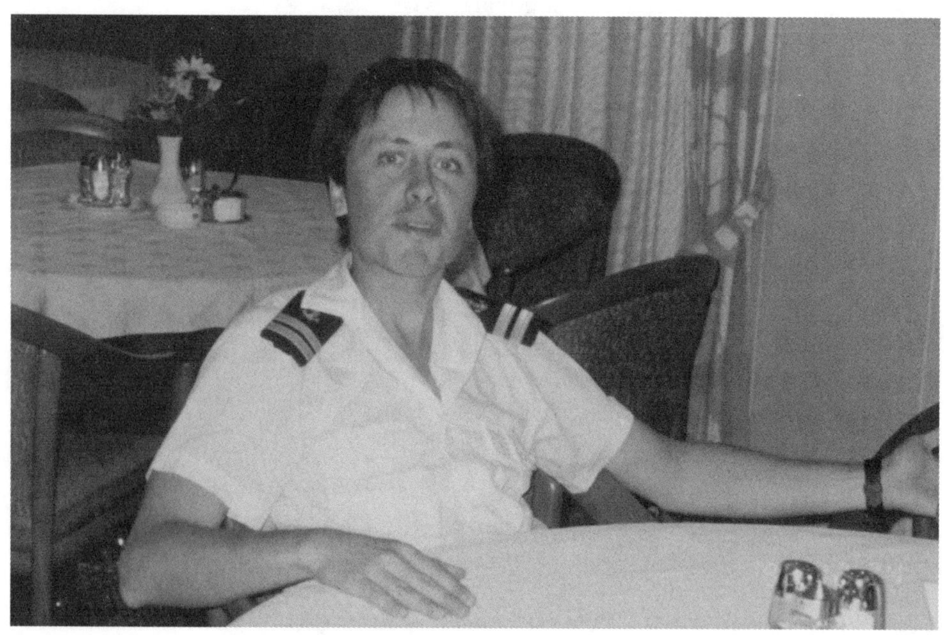

First Officer Marcello, from Argentina.

SHIP'S LOG

How to spend the "Golden Years" in comfort.

I was lucky to be shown this interesting area.

Even after a long tour of the museum, I found the huge salad to be too much.

again and we had breakfast. He is a fine cook. This day we drove to Virginia Beach to a retirement home where he has friends and hopes to live in a couple of years. This is Westminster Canterbury and resembles a plush hotel. The lobby and dining areas are spacious and are tastefully decorated. To be accepted as a resident, each must pay $100,000 and pass a health exam. This pays any medical costs that may be incurred the balance of one's life. Each resident must rent their own apartment and can cook there or eat in the dining room. Every comfort is available. There is a small store, theater, hair salon, swimming area, exercise gym and more.

We take a friend of Jack's, Sara, for a drive and go to the landing place where the English first landed on the North American continent. Also, he took me to the Episcopal Church where he was active for many years and to the graves of his parents. I was lucky to know someone who was willing to show me the area. The fall weather was perfect and the trees had not lost their colorful beauty. After the drive, we had a light meal and said goodbye again. He had a commitment in Richmond for Thanksgiving Day.

Before he left for Richmond he had arranged for my meals and transportation to the dock for the ship's arrival. His sister, Pat, took me to the Chrysler Museum for a tour of the glass displays. She knows a lot about glass and its history. I only know it is fascinating, particularly the original Tiffany lamps. We had lunch there and I ordered a salad. There must have been a whole head of lettuce as the base. I could only stare at it and knew no one could eat that many greens. It was a thrill to see this museum and it would have taken several more days to see it all.

That evening Jack's sister, Muriel, had a dinner party. It was fun to be invited and present were Pat and her hus-

SHIP'S LOG

It was a most memorable Thanksgiving Day.

He said that I'm authorized and welcome anytime.

I keep in touch with a some passengers.

band who is a farmer in the area and I. We dined on turkey, sweet potatoes, corn pudding, hot rolls, pie and white wine. Pat's husband, Bob, and I could talk some about farming. They grow winter wheat but are thinking of changing to cotton. It is a great expense for machinery to change the operation.

Next day Muriel and I went out for Thanksgiving dinner. The finest eating places were closed so we ate at a cafeteria and the food was excellent. We had a good day and I shall always remember it. She has an attractive southern accent and I just enjoyed listening to her. She is a dear. Next day we had a light lunch at a coffee house and off to the ship. These people would not let me pay for anything and I felt some guilt about that. There is no way to repay any of this.

My blood is pretty thick for this Miami heat. I have been welcomed with much warmth. I go up to the bridge and say hello to Pin. The door says "Authorized Personnel Only." The Captain says I am "authorized" and welcome any time. Some time ago Pin was opening a can of strong glue and some squirted in his eye. It was dangerous stuff and not known if his eye would ever be healed. Now Pin tells me it is almost normal again and Pin wants to know why Jack does not come to visit the ship anymore when they dock in Norfolk. I believe there is a reason and I am in the dark about it.

Jack now lives in a plush retirement home in Virginia Beach. This is Westminster Canterbury. He is one passenger with whom I stay in touch by mail or telephone. Also, I write to Dorothy Lane from London and Michael and Lynn Gasson from Western Australia.

One of the stewardesses named Raquel from Buenos Aires came bouncing into my cabin and plopped down

SHIP'S LOG

Raquel asks my advice about her love of two men.

There is a whole new cast of passengers.

Crude passengers are not appreciated on any cruise.

on the sofa. She can only be described as cute with black curls, dark eyes and loved to talk. She says she has such problems and is in love with two guys. One is Luise from Uruguay. He is not handsome or physical but has a warm heart. The other is Johann from Norway. He is very physical and handsome but is stand-offish and stoic. I can't advise her but tell her to think and consider a long time before she makes a decision. She talks a lot of her family, too. Her mother died two years ago of cancer. Raquel is outgoing and dear. I love it when she comes to visit.

The Messman, Malussie, is full of hugs and kisses. Even on the way to the lifeboat he is affectionate. We had a fire drill this morning. The Captain is not easy to get to know. He is not cold but just not outgoing. He is having a special dinner tomorrow night, November 30th.

We have sailed a long time by Cuba today on the starboard side. We are headed for Venezuela, the city of Puerto Cabello. There is a whole new cast of passengers. Some are definitely more enjoyable than others. One of the passengers I have traveled with before could not be more irritating. She has a gift for putting people down and making crude remarks. Maybe it is how she gets her kicks. She wants special food, special blankets and much attention. She hates her husband and comes on these trips alone.

After her insults of the evening in the presence of everyone at the dinner table, I eyeballed her and asked if she was trying to intimidate me. She said, "No, No, No!" I picked up my coffee and retired to my cabin. Carol, who is the wife of one of the officers, came to talk and comfort me but I was so offended my thinking was off base. She is bubbly and fun and I appreciated her visit. Isolda and Raquel came, too, and they bring me coffee and ice cream. This woman has been crude to two other passengers that I know about and the officers are not

happy about it. They have the right to put her off the ship if it becomes more pressing.

The Captain's dinner was tops with food and camaraderie. I tell him too much food and too much party. He says, "We haven't even got started!"

December 2nd, 1995

We are sailing out of the Port of La Guaira, Venezuela. This is near Caracas, the capital of the country and some of us took a tour into the city. We saw wealth, poverty, parliament, shops and terrible traffic. There are NO road rules. People everywhere. We had lunch at a good restaurant called the International Diner. There was much food including tenderloin with cheese, black beans and rice, salad and rolls. After all that, I couldn't eat dinner but had broth and coffee.

In this country the important historical hero is Simone Bolivar. Statues of him are very prominent. We are headed for Rio. This will take several days.

Svend comes to my cabin to appease me.

In the morning I walk to the bow. It is windy and my hair stands on end. Later, I wash my hair, roll it and it doesn't look like a salon hairdo but it must pass for awhile. The laundry is busy so I must wait to wash clothes. This is Sunday and Isolda brings me pizza, a hot dog and iced tea. I am not strong enough to go to the dining room after last night's insults from a bitch. Also, I have no interest in going to the cocktail hour. Svend comes to my cabin to appease me. I tell him I don't need to be where there are offensive remarks and discomfort. He says, "You is coming down for the social hour!"

I may have to be carried to the social hour.

I say, "No, I isn't!"

He says, "If you don't come down willingly I am going to physically carry you down."

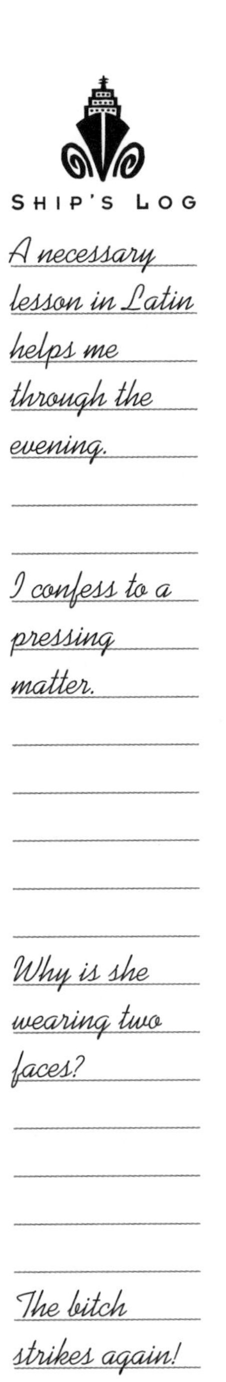

This could be quite exciting but I decline and agree to attend.

One passenger says to me, "Illigitimus Non Carborundum." Blankly I look at her and she tells me it is Latin for don't let the bastards grind you down.

Time to get to the laundry. Into the washer my clothes go. The water is so soft it is wise to use very little soap. The dryer had a shirt and trousers in it so I pressed those along with my blouses and pants. There were three of us in the laundry making jokes and having fun and we made bets on whose pants and shirt I pressed. Next day up at the bridge, Pin is wearing the very trousers and shirt I pressed. He was so surprised to find his clothes ironed and asked me if I knew who done it. I confessed.

The Equator Party on the deck was nice and everyone enjoyed it. There is a Brazilian drink made of rum, sugar, lime juice and ice. Be careful with it. The Bosun from Argentina played an accordion and people danced and sang. The passenger who throws out insults sat by me for a time but our conversation was clipped.

Isolda is having a problem. She and Raquel get along well together but in Buenos Aires Raquel is leaving the ship and another stewardess boards. Her name is Janeth. Isolda tells me she is a fine worker and pleasant to the passengers but is mean and says crude things to Isolda. Why do so many people wear two faces? Isolda tells me, "Maybe you have to help lift my moods until we reach New York."

One morning I find Isolda hunched over, quietly weeping in the dining room. She won't tell me why she weeps but points to the chair where the passenger sits and eats every meal. The same one who was so ungracious to me. I never did find out what happened between them

FiFi insults two other passengers for no reason at all.

We go to the Samba Show in Rio by water taxi.

It was a colorful show with lots of skin.

and Isolda told no one. She is truly a lady. This woman passenger who I call FiFi was nasty to two other passengers for no reason at all.

One of them was quiet, little Mia who never offended anyone and another was Nancy. Nancy is an interesting woman and on the ship to have fun. She handled the affronts with more ease than some of us. Nancy wore a beautiful black sheer shawl, studded with bits of gold, to the Captain's dinner. The shawl belonged to her grandmother and was special. It looked lovely with her dressy skirt and blouse. FiFi told her it looked ridiculous and why did she wear such a thing. Nancy could have slugged her but kept her cool. And so the story goes.

Anchored in the harbor at Rio were 17 ships waiting to dock. We waited some time before our turn. Svend had made reservations for some of us who wanted to go to the evening Samba Show. To get there we had to take the commuter boat or water taxi to the dock.

We waited and waited for it to come. Finally, Svend found out it had come and gone. The crew had taken it to shore. Svend was livid but he got another one to come. The shore taxi was waiting for us and we got to the show just on time. It began at 10:00 p.m..

The show was the most colorful I have ever seen. There were many dancers with beautiful bodies adorned in colored sequins, feathers, ribbons and beads. Some were barely adorned at all. The lovelier the body the more scantily clad they were. The show was suppose to tell the story of Brazilian history in music and dance. I have never seen that much skin at one time. Not even at the beach.

After the show we took a taxi to the dock where the water taxi was to pick us up and, lo and behold, it was not

Putting one's hair in rollers on a rolling ship is a real challenge.

The La Plata River is wide and polluted.

The Tango Show is fun to see again.

I like to see where I've been.

there. Svend said, "If the crew took our boat again they are in deep shit!" Soon though it did come and all ended well. It was a 20 minute ride to the ship. We sailed again sometime in the night.

Shampooing and putting rollers in your hair on a rolling ship can be a frustrating chore. I fell against the wall twice and was about to land on my butt but grabbed onto the sink and saved the fall. No one has called my hairdo Gravel Gertie yet, but maybe they are tempted.

It is so hot I told Svend I am lonesome for a sleigh ride in the snow. He offered to take me down to the freezer.

Sailing into Buenos Aires is a thrill. We sail on the La Plata River which is so wide that shore is not visible. The water has a brown, muddy cast. Closer in to the city the water looks black and has a terrible stink. Some is oil and the dregs of it. Argentina is just now beginning a few procedures to clean it up but there is little money available. The other passengers take a city tour but I have done that before and do not go again.

I will never tire of the Tango Show at the Casa Blanca and do attend once more. Argentine music is easy listening and has a beat, that for me, is spellbinding. There was a violinist, bass violin, viola, piano and concertina. The gauchos did their rope tricks and athletic twists and turns. I would be happy to see this show again and again.

My cabin has two windows on the starboard side and one aft. When containers are loaded at the stern it blocks my view of the wake of the ship. When I tell this to the Chief Mate he goes to look at it and has his papers along. He says the containers are to be unloaded at Salvador and if more are loaded, one can be left out to give me a peek hole. He had been the harbor captain in Santos which is

Instead of buying rocks, I should have had my head examined!

My sea legs are not so reliable on land.

We decorate the ship for Christmas.

a stressful job. After this trip, he will again resume the same job. He has the kindest face of any man on this ship. He has been at sea since he was 15 years old and could entertain all day with sea stories.

I am giving away some things I brought, thinking my suitcase will be lighter, and then I go to a rock shop in Rio Grande and buy stones. Should my head be examined? Maybe my suitcase will be stolen in New York and I won't have to deal with it. The rocks I bought come from the mine, are sliced thin and come in many colors. They are sold as wind chimes and make great gifts. They also come as pen holders and paper weights.

We must walk to the harbor gate as taxis are not allowed into the harbor area. When my feet get on land, everything goes topsy-turvy. My sea legs are not reliable on land. In Buenos Aires fresh flowers are brought to the cabins. There are white, red and pink roses. These are a delight and brighten the cabins. In Buenos Aires I received some mail. People in the U.S. are still thinking of me. All is well there.

The Captain does not wish to reach Salvador on Christmas Eve. If we are in port everyone has to work.

December 23rd

Many helped decorate for Christmas. There were 200 tiny new lights for the tree. Every year Harry, the electrician, throws them overboard because every year someone buys the wrong kind. After a lot of scurrying around he did find an adapter and got them to work. There was much grousing under his breath.

There were four people trimming the tree and they each spoke a different language. Each of us had to put on at least one decoration. It was such fun and the tree

Christmas Eve at sea is a cordial time.

Someone I really like makes me sneeze!

I have never seen so much food!

Our last stop before we head to New York.

looked elegant. Silver streamers hang from the ceiling and large snowflakes are dangling from them.

December 24th

We are at sea and there is socializing and everyone is cordial. Some gifts were exchanged. Ivaran gave each of us a pen and bags of candy. For Svend, I had an Edvard Grieg CD and other small items for the stewardesses. The special friend of an officer gave us each a rose.

Christmas Day

We were in Salvador and the crew and officers had to work. Therefore Christmas Day was observed December 26th. All were present except the First Mate who was at the bridge keeping us on course. Janeth had made a fake Santa Claus out of a full size suit, stuffing it with pillows, adding black boots, gloved hands and a long, white beard. I hugged Santa and his beard made me sneeze, it tickled so. Just when I meet someone I like a lot, I get the sneezes!

Christmas Day dinner was buffet and more food in one place I had never seen before. One room had the cold buffet and one room had the hot buffet. There were about 15 different salads, a whole baked salmon, a whole baked turkey, trays of liver paté, cheeses and meats. The hot buffet had pork loin, lamb, and prime rib plus 4 kinds of vegetables and deep-fried squid that to me looked like French Fried onions.

The Bosun is from Argentina. He played piano, accordion and we all sat around and sang the songs we knew. Some were in Spanish and some in English.

December 28th - Fortaleza Harbor, Brazil

This is our last stop until we head straight for New York. Most of us went into the city in the evening to the

SHIP'S LOG

It is heavenly to sit on the beach at night.

We get a good price on a taxi to the ship.

Svend didn't fare so well when he went back to the ship.

Pin yells, "Don't any-body move."

beach. We are almost on the equator and it is heavenly to sit on the beach at night. There is much for sale here for tourists. Tropical huts that look like jungle dwellings are numerous and from these snacks, soft drinks, and alcoholic drinks are sold.

Svend, Isolda and I sit awhile, drink rum and coke and watch people. She buys handmade pretty dresses for her little nieces. There is a busy street near us with large hotels and much traffic. The outdoor market sells countless items. Many are handmade. Some is perhaps good quality and some looks cheap. I don't buy anything. Children beg and that makes it difficult for me.

About 9:30 p.m. Isolda and I get a cab and return to the ship. She can speak fluent Portuguese and is a good bargainer so it cost very little for the taxi. Svend wanted to remain and find some of his fellow officers or crew members.

A short time later he crossed the street to get a taxi. Three thugs came up from behind and knocked him down, kicked him, took his watch and money. No one carries much money here. He had a black eye, bruises, and his ribs were sore the next day. The thugs ran off and some English-speaking people came to help him. If Svend had fought back they would have shot him. This was a surprise to be happening on such a busy street with many policemen around.

December 29th

We are to leave Fortaleza but there are many delays. A damaged container caused many hours of delay. About 8:00 p.m. I am in the Chief Mate's office with Fritz and Pin and alas! All the ship's electricity goes off. Pin goes into orbit and yells, "Don't anybody move. I must get to the Bridge!" He is thinking of all of his computers going

SHIP'S LOG

Another deck party provides time for reminiscing, music and song.

There are Port Captains and Harbor Masters.

The New Year is welcomed in, and the ship was rolling?

down. After a certain time had elapsed, the engineers got the standby generator going and a few lights are on, but not all. It takes an hour for the problem to be found and repaired. Since then, no emergencies have occurred but the Captain is frustrated and annoyed.

There is another deck party going north. I talked with Svend about past officers and crew. Captain Davidson of last year's trip is now Port Captain in Hamburg, Germany. Ernst, who resigned last year, is on another ship somewhere. First Mate Neilsen is the Captain on the Americana, also a freighter but carries many more passengers. Kjetel Vike is now the electrician on the Americana. Dimitri is on another ship. He liked to fight and did it once too often. Ron Andreason is no longer employed by Ivaran. He was too often into his cups. The fun of the deck party was the music provided by the Bosun and Antonio who sang many songs. They sang love songs, cry in your beer songs, sad songs and barroom songs. It was not a late party.

There is a difference between a Port Captain and Harbor Master. The Harbor Master is in charge of the whole Port. The Port Captain is responsible for freight and the correct loading of it for the company for whom he works.

December 31st.

There was, of course, another big gathering. There were snacks of many kinds, cocktails, dinner, coffee, brandy and chocolate. After all this, I walked Mia to her cabin. She would have fallen had I not caught her. There was some rolling for which we placed part of the blame. Nancy and I stayed at the party to welcome the New Year of 1996. We even toasted the New Year in Norway which was three hours earlier. About 11:30 the crew all came from the lower deck and Svend broke open the cham-

The difference between a fairy tale and a sea story.

There is good fellowship on this ship.

Was Cape Hatteras about to claim another ship?

The water was angry. Was it something I said?

pagne. At 12 midnight the kisses came from everywhere and we all had a jolly good time.

New Year's Day.

Everyone I see is walking around with their eyes half open, staring into space. There is an old saying about the difference between a sea story and a fairy tale. A fairy tale begins with "Once Upon A Time." A sea story begins with "This Ain't No Shit!"

Ivaran has four ships. Three of them sail this route between the U.S. and Argentina. One is the Santos which does not carry passengers. Another is the Americana which carries up to 80 passengers and is much more costly. There, dress for dinner is required and even for lunch, shorts are not acceptable. The third ship is the MV San Antonio; this is the one I sail with. Dress is very casual; as you please. There is much good fellowship on this ship. The fourth ship is the Santa Rosa. It carries no passengers and sails the Mediterranean.

There is a Captain's dinner as we are nearing the end of this trip. We dressed a little better and thoughts of packing and going home are uppermost in our minds. We were told it would be a straight, calm sail to New York. Not so. There was a vicious sea storm off Cape Hatteras. This is the place where many ships went down in years past and I thought we would be next.

The water was angry, the wind over 70 miles an hour. We rolled, pitched and jerked. It was impossible to be comfortable in bed without bracing the body somehow. This went on for 24 hours. Objects went flying across the cabin. One was the heavy, stainless steel water pitcher, books, pencils, papers and anything not anchored down. A bottle of pop rolled around in the frig, driving me crazy. I finally shoved it down between some cushions.

SHIP'S LOG

I got a severe headache but survived without broken bones.

A sad goodbye to Isolda and Pin.

The evening docking was not favored by passengers.

I ran like hell to the gate!

I managed to shower in the morning by hanging on with one hand. There was water all over the bathroom floor when I finished.

We were traveling five to seven knots which is about the speed of a bicycle. Many got sick. I do not get sick but a severe headache plagued me. It took four aspirins to take the edge off of it. It was time to pack. I spread open my suitcase, put in a garment and would have to sit and hold my head. Never before had I a headache like this. Packing was slow and laborious. Dishes crashed in the small galley off the dining room. Some passengers and crew have fallen but have no broken bones.

Saying goodbye was not so sad since I had not grown close to anyone even though I enjoyed them. It was saddest to say goodbye to Isolda and Pin. I believe Svend was happy to say goodbye to me as he had a whole new set of passengers boarding.

We had to leave the ship in the evening. The passengers were unhappy about this because none of us could get a flight that time of night. I was given a fax by the Captain that a reservation at a hotel was made near the airport and a reservation on Northwest Airlines next morning from Newark to Minneapolis to Fargo. When I arrived at Days Inn, there was no reservation but I did get a room. It was a cold morning of 13 below zero. The courtesy bus took me to the airport. I had to check in at the main desk because my ticket had been changed and it wasn't recorded in their computer. There was no reservation for me with the airline.

Time was short and I stood behind a woman who was planning a trip around the world and it seemed to take forever. As the plane was loading I did get waited on and ran like hell to get to the proper gate. I was scared and

angry but got a seat. Never in my life was I so happy to be on a plane headed west. This was only hours before the big snowstorm that tied up airports for several days. The angel on my shoulder was looking after me. Deplaning in Fargo was a wonderful relief even though the temperature was 18° below zero. All is well with me now.

Until I Saw the Sea

Lilian Moore

Until I saw the Sea,
I did not know
that wind
Could wrinkle water so.

I never knew
that sun
could splinter a whole sea of blue

Nor
did I know before
a sea breathes in and out
upon a shore.

Addendum

Here I offer information on freighter cruise companies for those who may be interested in taking a freighter cruise themselves. *Freighter World Cruises, Inc.*, the largest travel agency in the world dedicated to freighter travel, is the North American General Passenger Agent for the following lines. I have traveled with *Ivaran Lines*, and *Bergen Line*. The lines I've highlighted with a star are those that I would not hesitate to travel with.

- ★ *Bank Line*
- ★ *Chilean Line*
- • *Columbus Line*
- • *DSR – Deutsche Seereederei Rostock*
- • *Doehle Line*
- • *Dollart Line*
- • *Egon Oldendorff*
- • *Grimaldi Line*
- • *F. Laeisz Line*
- • *Leonhardt & blumberg*
- • *Martime Reederei*
- • *MC Shipping*
- ★ *Mineral Shipping*
- • *NSB – Niederelbe Schiffahrtsgesellschaft Buxtehude*
- • *Projex Line*
- • *Schepers Line*
- • *Schlüter Line*
- • *Reederei Bernhard Schulte*
- • *Transeste Shipping*

Freighter World Cruises also represents the following lines:

- ★ *Ivaran Lines*
- • *Compagnie Polynesienne de Transport Maritime*
- ★ *Bergen Line*
- • *Safmarine*
- • *United Baltic Corp.*
- • *St. Helena Shipping Line*
- • *Horn Linie*
- • *Blue Star*
- • *Canada Maritime*

Freighter World Cruises, Inc.
180 South Lake Avenue, Suite 335
Pasadena, CA 91101-3106, USA
Telephone: 800-531-7774 or 626-449-3106
Fax: 626-449-9573 E-mail: freighters@earthlink.net